CREATIVE ANALYSIS

CREATIVE ANALYSIS

Revised Edition

by Albert Upton, Richard W. Samson, and Ann Dahlstrom Farmer

Design, Photography, and Art Direction by J. F. Youngstrom, Jr.
Illustrations by Rex John Irvine

A Sunrise Book
E. P. DUTTON
NEW YORK

Special acknowledgments are due to Joseph Lawrence, who edited the manuscript, and to Joseph Youngstrom, who designed the book and supervised the illustration and typography. We are indebted to Rex Irvine for the illustrations.

Joan Karetov deserves thanks for drawing the diagrams and preparing the copy for the printer. We are grateful to Jeanette Miller for checking the proofs and offering editorial suggestions. Gilbert McEwen, Fred Harrison, and Mary Nash deserve thanks for their recommendations in the preparation of the manuscript. We are also indebted, for their various contributions, to Opal Shultz, Dennis Kilgo, Donna Helt, Irene Cantu, Susan Winner, Peggy Kinzer, Dawn Duncan, Sally McEwen, Lane Stuart, Heather Stuart, Dianne Stuart, and Les Heather.

For information contact: E.P. Dutton, 2 Park Avenue, New York, N.Y. 10016

Library of Congress Cataloging in Publication Data

Upton, Albert.
    Creative analysis.

    1. Problem solving—Problems, exercises, etc.   2. Creative thinking—Problems, exercises, etc.   I. Samson, Richard W., joint author.   II. Farmer, Ann Dahlstrom, joint author.   III. Title.
    BF455.U66 1978   153.43   77-28766

ISBN: 0-87690-281-6

Published simultaneously in Canada by Clarke, Irwin & Company Limited, Toronto and Vancouver

10   9   8   7   6   5   4   3   2   1

First Revised Edition

Creative Analysis, largely the work of Richard Samson, was composed in 1960 as a workbook for Albert Upton's *Design for Thinking,* which was used in the required first-year English program established at Whittier College in 1938. Widespread publicity that followed a front-page article by Fred M. Hechinger in the *New York Times* of June 27, 1960, prompted the Stanford University Press to publish the seventh edition of *Design for Thinking* in 1961 * and E. P. Dutton and Company to publish the second edition of *Creative Analysis* in 1963. Since then, *Creative Analysis* has been used in schools, colleges, universities, professional schools, and government, as well as in individual self-education.

The effectiveness of the method we present has been attested to over the years on numerous occasions and in various ways. We have been particularly gratified by the pretest-posttest differentials recorded by Dr. Eugene Brunelle of St. Mary's College, Maryland, on both IQ and creativity tests. We believe that creativity scores are influenced by the essential prominence of the sensory and affective factors present in the analysis of metaphor.

It is not generally realized that there are two sorts of symbols: natural and artificial. We apparently share the natural with the rest of the higher animals, but conventional symbols such as language and musical notation are artifacts made by us humans to meet our human needs and to gratify our human desires. These exercises and the principles they demonstrate are designed to improve the cognitive or logical function of the brain, but our experience with ten college generations has made it clear that enhancement of the sensory and emotional functions is a by-product as the individual becomes aware of the various relations between language and life. Such an awareness necessarily provides the expanded vocabulary each person needs to act knowledgeably in the modern world. What most of us fail to see is the corresponding necessity of growth in the sets of senses of the familiar words we know best.

---

* Now in paperback: Pacific Books, Palo Alto, CA 94302.

The publisher's request for a revised edition finds Richard Samson preoccupied as director of creativity at Economics Press of Fairfield, New Jersey. We therefore welcome the partnership of Ann Farmer, who is the present director of the Whittier College program. Ann Farmer's training (M.A.s in linguistics and sociology), her editorial experience, and years of active participation in the systematic use of *Creative Analysis* precisely qualify her for the task at hand. Albert Upton is still an active consultant in the field.

It is a privilege and delight to thank members of the Whittier English department—Arnold Chadderdon, Roberta Forsberg, Anne Kiley, and Gilbert McEwen—for their participation in the program, and, in particular, William Geiger, for his aid with the revised manuscript. Malcolm Farmer, director of the Whittier Learning Resources Center, has been a constant help in both work and counsel. They have all contrived, with vigorous student support, to maintain a fairly rigorous discipline in an era of scholastic permissiveness.

A good dictionary is a must. We recommend possession of or convenient access to the *American Heritage Dictionary,* the *Random House Dictionary, Webster's Collegiate Dictionary,* or *Webster's New World Dictionary.*

—A.U., R.W.S., and A.D.F.

Contents

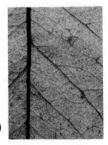

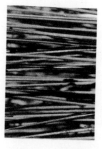

CREATIVE ANALYSIS

QUALIFICATION

SECTION 1

THINGS AND QUALITIES

TEXT

Thinking is a skill we have to learn by the trial-and-error method we call practice. It must be, for the most part, the product of conscious experience. Conscious experience is made up of sensation, emotion, and the perception of similarity and difference, which in human beings becomes the power of abstraction. The partial storage of experience called memory is, of course, essential to the thinking process.

Now language and its related symbol systems are not natural but are artifacts invented by humankind to facilitate and preserve conscious experience. Language functions not only as an instrument of communication but as a means of expressing or controlling emotion and, above all, as the chief instrument of the thinking skill called problem solving or analysis.

We have good reason for coupling the terms *creative* and *analysis* in our title. We tend to associate the first term with art and the other with science. It is our hope that in working these exercises you will see more clearly that the two cooperate in the problem-solving process. The "taking apart" of analysis may well be the necessary beginning of a new "putting together," or creative synthesis.

There are three kinds of analysis—*classification analysis, structure analysis,* and *operation analysis;* they are all logical operations in which symbols play the definitive role. We shall begin with the concepts of *thing* and *quality,* because they are basic to all rational procedures, and with the classification method, because it is the rational procedure we all use most often and is the easiest to understand.

A *thing* is anything that may be thought of as having substance bounded by limits of space *or* space and time. Suppose you are given this collection of things bounded by limits of space and asked to name them and group them according to their similarities and differences:

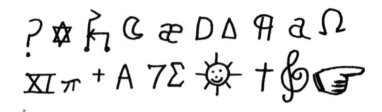

Each of these things can be described by listing its various qualities—its shape, its field of use, and so forth. All of these things have at least one quality in common, making them members of one group; other qualities may or may not be shared with any other member. They are variously similar to and different from one another.

Try the following procedure to note *systematically* the similarities and differences among these things.

1. Write a name for the entire group.
2. Ask the question, What are the *main* sorts of these things? The answer will be relevant to the problem at hand. A landscape architect doesn't sort plants according to their genetic relations, as a botanist does. In this case our purpose is merely to illustrate *classification.* We could say that these things are printed characters that are either arbitrary or representative in form and show this in a diagram:

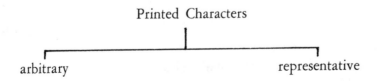

3. Continue to ask, What are the main sorts of each sort? until you have separated the items sufficiently for your purpose.

4. Make a horizontal line at the lower end of every vertical line that represents a group to be further subdivided. Each such line represents the quality or respect in which the two or more species below it differ, * hence we call it a *horizontal sorting factor.* Our main sorts of printed characters, "arbitrary" and "representative," differ according to the method of symbolization—according to whether they look like the things they stand for or not. We could write "method of symbolization" in parentheses on the horizontal line.

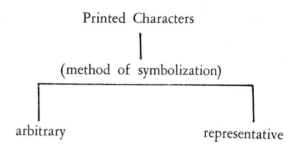

5. Make vertical lines between the horizontal levels. Each vertical line represents the quality which all the branches and/or items below it have in common; hence we call these *vertical sorting factors.* "Arbitrary" is a vertical sorting factor because all the branches and items below that heading have the quality of arbitrariness in common.

---

* Note that we might have used *quality* alone or *respect* alone; thus, *respect* is a synonym for *quality* and might then be defined as a "relevant quality." And thus you see that a quality may have a quality.

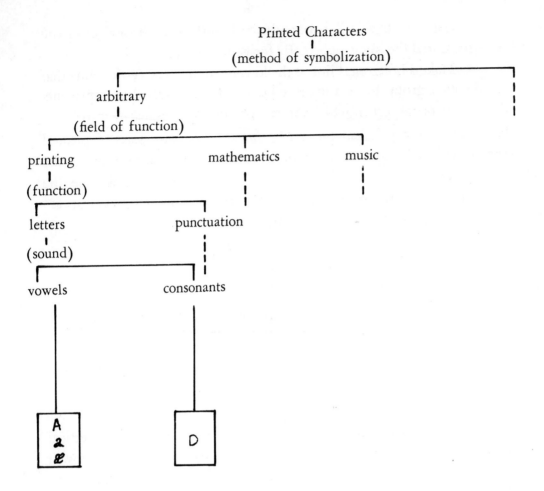

6. Make boxes, or pigeonholes, to represent the levels that contain the things themselves or symbols that stand for the things. In this type of classification a pigeonhole may contain one, few, or many "pigeons," depending on our purpose. There are no vacant holes because the collection is closed.

Thus a finished classification of these things might look like this:

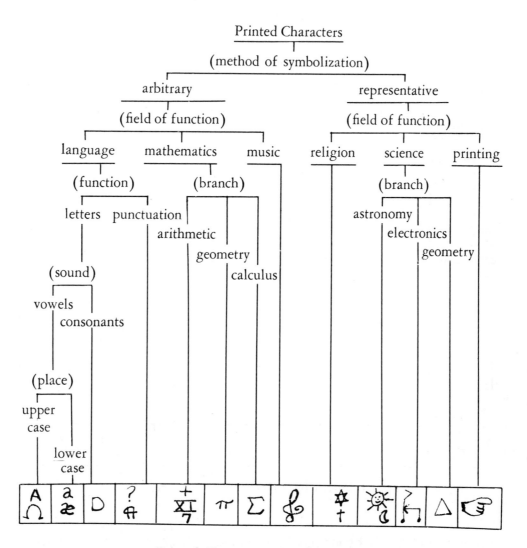

Printed Characters Classification #1

Or this:

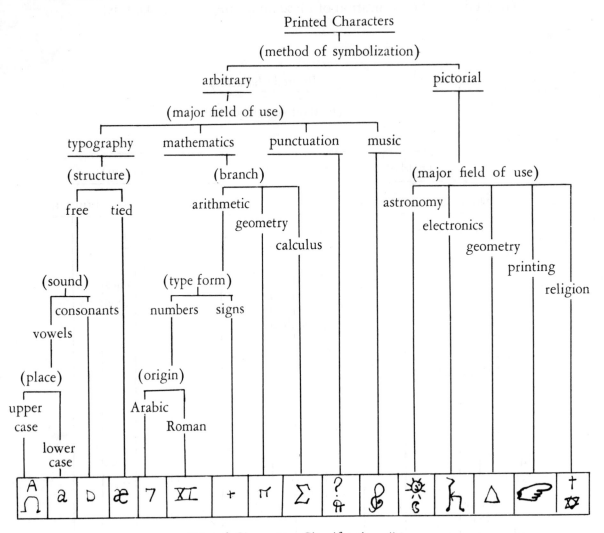

Printed Characters Classification #2

It is quite possible that your classification differs from ours in the number of levels, in the number of sorts, and/or in the terms themselves. A classification is "right" to the degree that it names qualities relevant to the purpose and names enough qualities to fulfill that purpose.

Remember, when you go to work on your own classifications, work down from the top, keeping in mind: What are the main sorts in this branch at this level, and what quality am I sorting according to? Do not waste time designing a neat diagram. Use plenty of paper so that your diagram may grow. The neatness may come later if you wish, but the fundamental purpose is to order your thoughts so you can make up your mind.

1•1•2

EXERCISES

1. Answer the following questions concerning the Printed Characters classifications.
   A. Which levels deal with qualities, which with things?
      Printed Characters Classification #1—
      Qualities: ——————————————————————————
      Things: ——————————————————————————
      Printed Characters Classification #2—
      Qualities: ——————————————————————————
      Things: ——————————————————————————
   B. Classification #1 has 28 sorting factors. List them beneath the appropriate headings below.

   Vertical   *Horizontal*

   —————————— ——————————   —————————— ——————————
   —————————— ——————————   —————————— ——————————
   —————————— ——————————   —————————— ——————————
   —————————— ——————————   —————————— ——————————
   —————————— ——————————   —————————— ——————————
   —————————— ——————————   —————————— ——————————
   —————————— ——————————   —————————— ——————————
   —————————— ——————————   —————————— ——————————
   —————————— ——————————   —————————— ——————————

Classification #2 has 33 sorting factors. List them beneath the appropriate headings below.

Vertical   *Horizontal*

——————— ———————   ——————— ———————
——————— ———————   ——————— ———————
——————— ———————   ——————— ———————
——————— ———————   ——————— ———————
——————— ———————   ——————— ———————
——————— ———————   ——————— ———————
——————— ———————   ——————— ———————
——————— ———————   ——————— ———————
——————— ———————   ——————— ———————

C. In Classification #1, which sorting factor indicates a way in which Ꞧ , ɑ, and ƻ are similar? ——————————
In Classification #2, which sorting factor indicates the similarity?

——————————

In Classification #1, which sorting factor indicates a way in which ﬀ and ᴅ are similar? ——————————
In Classification #2, which sorting factor indicates the similarity?

——————————

What kind of sorting factors are these? ——————————

D. In Classification #1, which sorting factor indicates the kinds of differences between *arbitrary* and *representative?* ——————————
In Classification #2, which sorting factor indicates the kinds of differences between *arbitrary* and *pictorial?* ——————————
What kind of sorting factors are these? ——————————

2. Is the printer's use of the word *fist* illegitimate? What determines the legitimacy of a usage? May a use that is born illegitimate ever be truly legitimate?

3. Choose 10 additional things at random from the symbols and signs chart in your dictionary and add them to your classification. What changes in sorting factors did you need to make?

4. When a classification has but two main sorts or categories, it is called a *dichotomy.* How would you dichotomize the books in a typical household collection? What sort of sorting factors did you use?

5. On a separate sheet of paper, make a classification-analysis diagram of the contents of a desk drawer or a bag of grocery items.

1*2

MODES OF CONSCIOUSNESS

1*2*1

TEXT

The three components of consciousness—sensation, emotion, and reason —yield us the useful concept of *mode*. Complete thoughts usually have at least a trace of each, but when, for example, one of them—say, emotion—is dominant, we speak of the thought as being in the affective mode; the other two components determine the sensory and logical modes. This concept is not only useful in analyzing the behavior of others but in promoting an awareness of the nature of our own thinking. Perceiving the color of an object, listening to music, feeling the heat of the sun, stroking the fur of a cat, and seeing a bouquet of flowers are examples of a predominantly sensory mode of consciousness. Feeling sad or angry, disliking someone or something, and feeling that a bouquet of flowers is beautiful primarily involve the affective mode of consciousness. Adding two and two, noticing that one building is higher than another or farther away, determining that a ball is made of rubber, and analyzing an arrangement of flowers illustrate the logical mode of consciousness.

1*2*2

EXERCISES

1. Write an *S, A,* or *L* in each blank space below, indicating whether the statement refers primarily to a sensory, affective, or logical mode of consciousness. The names of key qualities have been italicized. The statements come from Thomas Hardy's *Return of the Native* or *The Mayor of Casterbridge.*

   S   a. Thursday . . . was one of a series of days during which snug houses were *stifling,* and when *cool* draughts were treats. . . .

   L   b. *One* evening of *late* summer, before the *nineteenth* century had reached *one-third* its span. . . .

   A   c. A *fair, sweet,* and *honest* country face was revealed. . . . It was between *pretty* and *beautiful.*

   S   d. . . . *brown* corduroy . . . *white* horn buttons . . . *black* glazed canvas.

   L   e. As the resting man looked at the barrow he became aware that its summit, hitherto the *highest* object in the whole round, was surmounted by something *higher.*

   L   f. Wildeve is *older* than Tamsin Yeobright by a . . . *few* summers.

   A   g. The groundwork of the face was *hopefulness;* but over it now lay like a foreign substance a film of *anxiety* and *grief.*

   S   h. She was a woman *noisily* constructed; in addition to her enclosing framework of whalebone and lath, she wore pattens summer and winter, in wet weather and in dry, to preserve her boots from wear; and when Fairway began to [dance] about with her, the *clicking* of the pattens, the *creaking* of the stays, and her *screams* of surprise, formed a very *audible* concert.

_L_ i. A road neither *straight* nor *crooked,* neither *level* nor *hilly.* . . .

_S_ j. The heaven being spread with this *pallid* screen and the earth with the *darkest* vegetation. . . .

_A_ k. . . . and being a man of the *mournfullest* make, I was *scared* a little, that's all.

_L_ l. At the *upper* end stood a stove . . . *over* which hung a *large three-legged* crock sufficiently polished round the rim to show that it was made of *bell-metal.*

_A_ m. At the end of the first [cup] the man had risen to *serenity;* at the second he was *jovial;* at the third, *argumentative.* . . .

_L_ n. The garden was *at* the back, and *behind* this ran a *still deep* stream, forming the margin of the heath *in* this direction, meadowland appearing *beyond* the stream.

2. On a separate sheet of paper describe three sensory, three affective, and three logical modes of consciousness which you have experienced.

3. In a novel, short story, poem, or other piece of writing, find descriptions of a sensory, an affective, and a logical mode of consciousness.

1*3

THE NAMING OF QUALITIES

1*3*1

TEXT

The naming of qualities takes place within consciousness. Although consciousness is an integration—a making into one—of sensation, emotion, and logic, individual qualities may be abstracted from total experiences. You can experience an apple. It is a *structure* bounded by space, a physical object, a thing. You can see it, smell it, heft it. Eating it is also a thing—an *operation* bounded by space *and* time. Both you and the apple (structures) have to move; change takes place in time. Suppose it is a large, firm, sweet, juicy, delicious Delicious. These are all qualities that the apple has, because they are all names of the different sorts that the apple can be. *Qualis* means "sort" in Latin; *qualification* means "making of a sort." Our sensory-affective-logical triad yields us one useful answer to the question, What sorts of sorts are there? In what mode would you put the foregoing apple description, and how would you sort each word in it? Are all Delicious apples delicious, and could a Winesap be delicious? What qualities would put Jonathans in the same group as Winesaps and Delicious? What qualities make them neither Winesaps nor Delicious?

Below are more examples of sorts of sensory, affective, and logical qualifications. In actual use a single word may represent a combination of several of the psychological components listed here.

QUALIFICATIONS

SENSORY QUALIFICATIONS:

1. VISION   Words such as *red, yellow, blue, green,* and *brown* may be color qualifications. Words such as *light, bright, blinding, dark, dull,* and *dim* may be brightness qualifications.

2. HEARING   *Shrill, medium,* and *deep* may be examples of tone qualifications. Intensity qualifications may be words such as *loud* and *soft.* Complex sound experiences may have names such as *piercing, brassy,* and *hoarse.*

3. SMELL   Here are some words which may be general smell qualifications: *fragrant, fetid, stink, sweet, bad, aroma, bouquet.* Specific smell qualifications are usually words borrowed from the assumed source of the odor. Some examples are *rose, sulphurous, pine,* and *mint.*

4. TASTE   *Sweet, sour, salty, bitter, savory,* and *delicious* may be taste qualifications.

5. BALANCE   *Lean, stable, giddy, dizzy,* and *poise* may symbolize sensations that may possibly originate in the equilibratory mechanism of the internal ear.

6. SKIN   Skin qualifications are the names of "touch" and temperature responses. "Touch" qualifications may be words such as *burn, itch, tickle, smart, titillate, caress, creep, shudder, tingle, smooth, rough, sharp,* and *velvet.* Temperature qualifications may be words such as *hot, cold, cool, chill, warm,* and *cozy.*

7. MUSCLE   *Squeeze, hug, jam, press,* and *push* may be names of sensations of deep pressure. *Heavy, heft, strain, stretch, cramp, twist, pull, taut,* and *loose* may be names of sensations of tension in the muscles, tendons, and joints.

The above list is by no means a comprehensive summary of all sensory qualifications. Our vocabularies of sensation also include words such as *hungry, thirsty, nauseated, tired, ache, hurt, stuffy, dull, exhilaration, suffocating, flushed, panicky, thrill, ecstasy, wanton, voluptuous, full, stuffed, piercing,* and *sharp.*

1. LOVE   Feelings of love may be symbolized by words such as *loving, dear, darling, warm, sweet, tender, affection, attraction, infatuation, devotion,* and *liking.*

2. JOY   *Happy, pleasant, glad, delighted, joyful, gratified,* and *exuberant* may be qualifications of joy.

3. AWE (WONDER)   Qualifications of awe or wonder may be words such as *amazing, wondrous, majestic, sublime, profound, grand, sacred, marvelous, astonishing, surprising, strange,* and *incredible.*

4. ANGER   Feelings of anger may be signified by words such as *angry, mad, furious, heated, indignant, wrath, rage,* and *ire.*

5. FEAR   *Terrified, afraid, alarmed, frightened, apprehensive, dreadful,* and *frantic* may symbolize emotions of fear.

6. SORROW   Words such as *sad, sorrowful, grief, regret, mourning, lamentation, anguish,* and *woe* may be qualifications of sorrow.

7. BEAUTY   *Beautiful, ugly, lovely, good-looking, plain, fair, offensive, unsightly, comely, pretty, cute, grotesque, handsome, attractive,* and *repulsive* may be qualifications of beauty or its opposite.

The qualifications listed above are names of some of our more basic emotions. Here are some terms which may specify other emotional states: *courageous, curious, funny, humiliated, mysterious, scorn, frustration, related (belonging), bitter, disgust, envy, inferior, foolish, sympathetic, uncertain, victorious, shame, secure, hate, bored, modest, anxiety, lonely, certain, hope,* and *shocked.*

LOGICAL QUALIFICATIONS:

1. NUMBER   Qualities of number may be signified by terms such as *one, two, three, twelve, one hundred and nineteen, first, second, fiftieth, last, none, some, all, few,* and *many.*

2. MAGNITUDE (SIZE)   Magnitude qualifications signify qualities of dimension, area, and volume. Words such as *little, small, tiny, miniature, big, large, huge, mammoth, long, short, high, tall, slim, wide,* and *narrow* may be magnitude qualifications.

3. STRUCTURE (SHAPE)   Structure or shape qualifications may be words such as *contour, form, figure, arrangement, straight, angular, round, organization, interrelation, spherical, square, bent, oval,* and *spiral.*

4. SUBSTANCE (MATTER AND/OR ENERGY)   A word is a substance qualification to the extent that it signifies the unseen "essential element" of a thing. The word *sand* is a substance qualification to the extent that it symbolizes the essential "ingredient" of sand, apart from its color or texture. Substance qualifications may be words such as *steel, iron, metal, light, electricity, water, liquid, paint, dirt, alcohol, glass, air,* and *hydrogen.*

5. TIME   *Duration, moment, interval, instant, second, minute, hour, day, year, now, past, present, future, then, when, long, short, during, after, before, early, late, between, still,* and *since* may be time qualifications.

6. SPACE   Space qualifications may be terms such as *direction, orientation, position, location, in, up, down, on, between, far, near, North, here, there, out, over, under, right, left,* and *upside down.*

7. CHANGE   Change qualifications are general terms. Other logical qualifications often signify dimensions of change. Thus we may speak of change in number, change in size, change in structure, and so forth. Examples of change qualifications may be *modify, alter, convert, transform, vary, affect, improve, cause,* and *effect.*

Many logical qualifications represent combinations of basic logical qualities. *Motion,* for example, may mean *change* in *space.* Here are some terms which for the most part, in most contexts, represent combinations of two or more basic logical qualities: *regular, velocity, complex, simple, opposite, force, elastic, free, frequent, general, particular, new, solid, open, fast, parallel, possible, separate, sudden, young, complete, similar, different,* and *constant (unchanging).*

In conclusion we may say that the first six logical qualifications are dimensions or manifestations of the seventh. Something may change in respect to any or all of the six.

EXERCISES

1*3*2*1

BASIC QUALIFICATIONS

In the following exercise the items are phrases in which italicized words are used as the names of basic qualities. In the first column after the items, write whether each quality is sensory, affective, or logical. In the second column indicate the sort of sensory, affective, or logical quality it is. Some items are ambiguous; the particular definition will determine the placement. When you have finished, make a classification-analysis diagram of either the sensory, the affective, or the logical qualities. The first two items have been done for you.

	Main Sort	Subsort
1. A *sour* apple	sensory	taste
2. A *round* object	logical	structure
3. A *loving* smile		
4. A *small* man		
5. *Seven* months		
6. A *red* dress		
7. *Fragrant* flowers		
8. An *angry* mob		
9. *In* the pot		
10. *Smooth* wood (to the touch)		
11. *Early* in the morning		
12. *A* man		
13. A *shrill* whistle		
14. A *steel* rod		
15. *Future* mistakes		
16. A *happy* man		
17. *Up*stream		
18. A *late* apology		
19. *By* the door		
20. A *straight* line		
21. *Before* marriage		
22. A *bright* star		
23. *On* the floor		
24. A *big* dog		
25. Hot-*air* balloon		
26. *During* the performance		
27. *One* possibility		
28. An *amazing* feat		
29. *Plastic* coating		
30. A *few* dollars		
31. *When* it snows		
32. A *hard* ball (to squeeze)		

	Main Sort	Subsort
33. *Between* two trees		
34. An *angular* house		
35. A *cold* drink		
36. Until *then*		
37. A ray of *light*		
38. *Far* from home		
39. A *frightened* child		
40. A *cotton* dress		
41. A *tiny* elephant		
42. A *dizzy* ride		
43. A *thousand* reasons		
44. *North* of Detroit		
45. An *altered* mechanism		
46. A *sad* moment		
47. *In* preparation		
48. A *spherical* ornament		
49. A *beautiful* flower		
50. A *yellow* sun		
51. A *paper* cup		
52. A *sweet* fig		
53. An *ugly* sight		
54. *An* apple		
55. A *delightful* experience		
56. *Many* opportunities		
57. *Stinking* garbage		
58. A *furious* dog		
59. A *little* car		
60. A *loud* crash		
61. A *grieving* mother		
62. In *here*		
63. An *electric* current		
64. A *dark* shadow		
65. Starting *now*		
66. *Rough* sand (to walk on barefoot)		
67. A *stable* posture		
68. A *wondrous* sight		
69. *An egg-shaped* head		

	Main Sort	*Subsort*
70. *Still* whispering	_____	_____
71. A *heavy* stone (to lift)	_____	_____
72. A *dear* friend	_____	_____
73. A *deep* voice	_____	_____
74. A *large* mouse	_____	_____
75. A *warm* day	_____	_____
76. A *terrified* soldier	_____	_____
77. *Out* of the house	_____	_____
78. A *soft* whisper	_____	_____
79. A *spiral* stairway	_____	_____
80. A *lovely* girl	_____	_____
81. A *converted* factory	_____	_____
82. A *sorrowful* loss	_____	_____
83. A *bitter* pill	_____	_____
84. A *sand* castle	_____	_____
85. *Blue* eyes	_____	_____
86. *Some* eggs	_____	_____
87. A *transformed* attitude	_____	_____
88. *Sticky* paste	_____	_____
89. An *alarmed* community	_____	_____
90. A *falling* sensation	_____	_____
91. A *variable* procedure	_____	_____
92. *Until* May	_____	_____
93. A *tight* muscle	_____	_____
94. A *delicious* meal	_____	_____
95. *Over* her shoulder	_____	_____
96. An *indignant* wife	_____	_____
97. A *dim* taillight	_____	_____
98. *Hot* tea	_____	_____
99. *After* the play	_____	_____
100. *Pleasant* company	_____	_____

1*3*2*2

ABSTRACTION OF QUALITIES FROM THINGS

On a separate sheet of paper name three sensory, three affective, and three logical qualities of each of the *things* indicated below.

1

2

3

4

5

6

7

8

9   10

THE RELATIONSHIP BETWEEN QUALIFICATION AND CLASSIFICATION

TEXT

In working with words like *thing* and *quality,* we must keep in mind that we are thinking about consciousness; we must *re*mind ourselves that the words *mind, thought,* and *consciousness* may, in fact, be synonyms. It follows that everything is a thing that exists in the mind because thoughts are things (operations). But we still have to tell them apart, because one thought can be about another thought. *Jimmy Carter is now our president* might be called a *complete thought* made of three *part-thoughts:* a *subject thought,* a *space-time thought,* and an *office thought. Jimmy Carter* would then refer to a "thing" and the other two would be "qualities" of that thing. If you were to say, "There is the president," then *president* would refer to a thing and *there is* would refer to the quality of being in space and time. And so we may conclude that the word *president* may refer to an abstract thing—the office—and a concrete thing—Jimmy Carter.

We may say that all qualities are abstract because the mind "abstracts" them from the things that "have" them, but that does not mean that the word *quality* always stands for a quality. Just as the office of president, or the presidency, is an abstract thing and the "oval office" is a concrete thing, so the *quality* of Georgia is a concrete group of people and Georgian social status is an abstract thing.

1 * 4 * 2

EXERCISES

Give a name to each group of things pictured below. Then list two ways in which they are similar and two ways in which they are different.

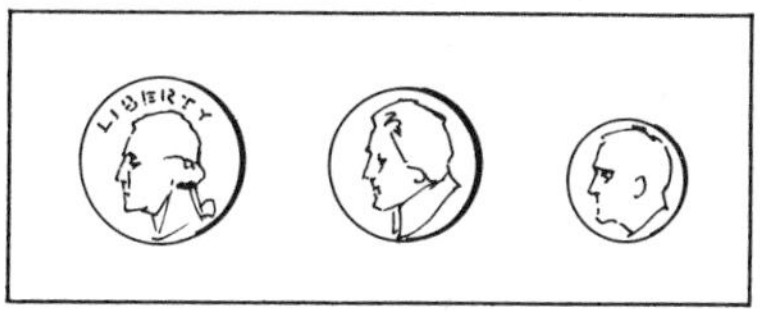

name _____ **1**

similar _____ different _____
_____ _____

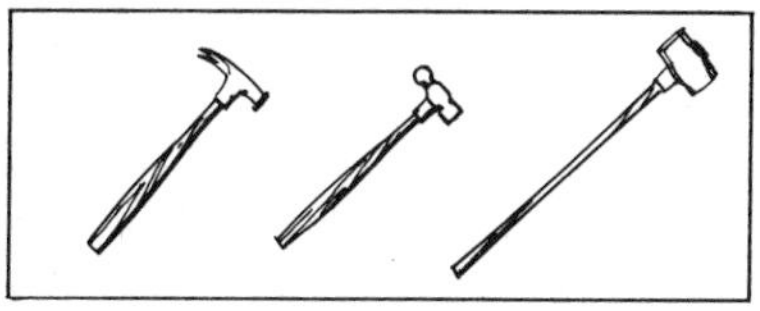

name _____ **2**

similar _____ different _____
_____ _____

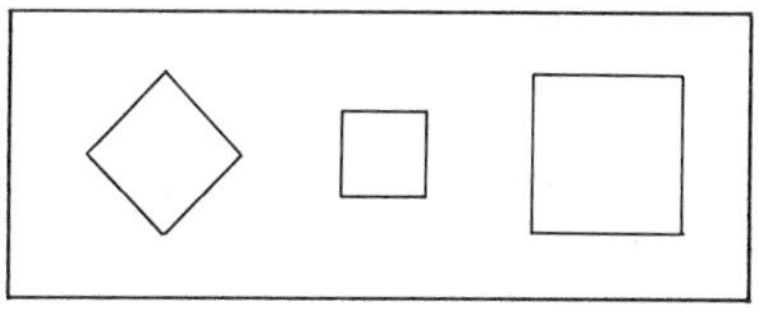

name _____ **3**

similar _____ different _____
_____ _____

name _____ **4**

similar _____ different _____
_____ _____

name _____ **5**

similar _____ different _____
_____ _____

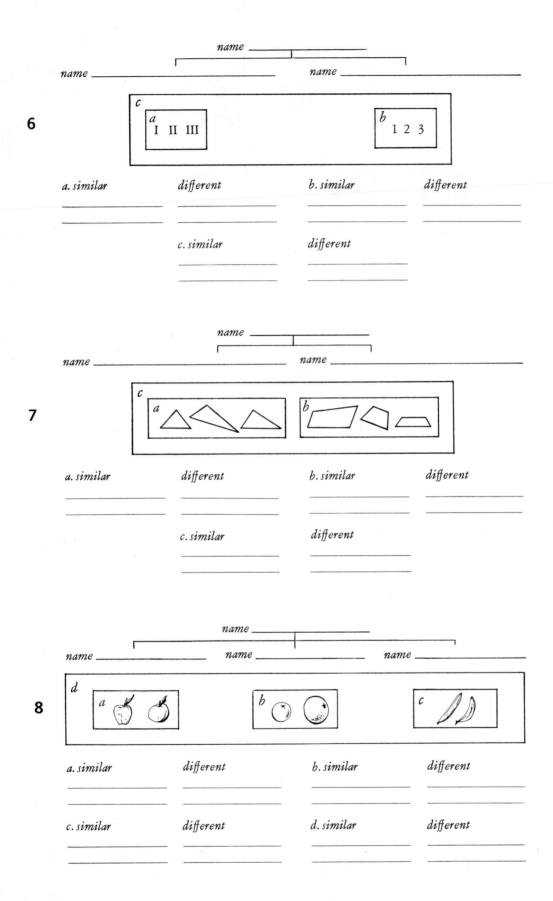

6

name _____

name _____   name _____

a. similar   different   b. similar   different

_____ _____ _____ _____
_____

              c. similar   different

              _____ _____
              _____ _____

7

name _____

name _____   name _____

a. similar   different   b. similar   different

_____ _____ _____ _____
_____ _____ _____ _____

              c. similar   different

              _____ _____
              _____ _____

8

name _____

name _____   name _____   name _____

a. similar   different   b. similar   different

_____ _____ _____ _____
_____ _____ _____ _____

c. similar   different   d. similar   different

_____ _____ _____ _____
_____ _____ _____ _____

name _____

name _____   *name* _____

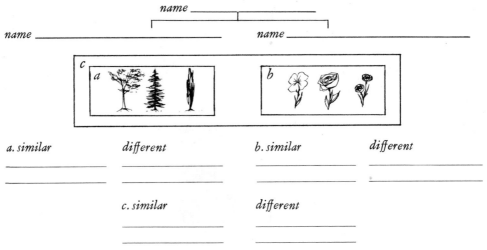

a. *similar*   *different*   b. *similar*   *different*

_____   _____   _____   _____

_____   _____   _____   _____

c. *similar*   *different*

_____   _____

_____   _____

name _____

name _____   *name* _____

name _____   *name* _____   *name* _____   *name* _____

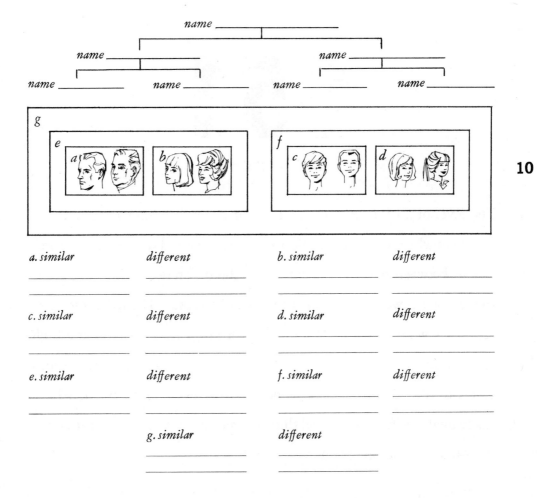

10

a. *similar*   *different*   b. *similar*   *different*

_____   _____   _____   _____

_____   _____   _____   _____

c. *similar*   *different*   d. *similar*   *different*

_____   _____   _____   _____

_____   _____   _____   _____

e. *similar*   *different*   f. *similar*   *different*

_____   _____   _____   _____

_____   _____   _____   _____

g. *similar*   *different*

_____   _____

_____   _____

1*5

LEVELS OF ABSTRACTION

1*5*1

TEXT

The level of abstraction (or the level of generalization) is the relative degree to which things as symbolized are similar and different. The similarities between two ants far outweigh the differences. The opposite is the case when we compare an ant with a eucalyptus. The word *ant* operates at a low level of abstraction. The word *organism* operates at a high level of abstraction. *Hen, chicken, fowl,* and *animal* operate at various levels of abstraction. Things named at low levels of abstraction have many qualities in common and things named at high levels of abstraction have few qualities in common.

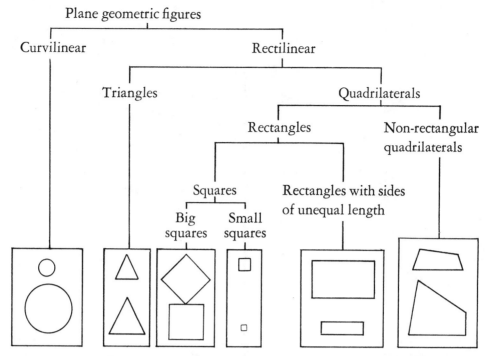

Big squares, in the diagram above, are similar in all respects except position. Squares differ not only in position but also in size. Rectangles differ in position, size, and certain aspects of shape. Quadrilaterals are alike only in respect of being plane figures with four straight sides. The level of abstraction is determined by the relative proportion of similarities and differences among the things signified. The higher the level of abstraction, the greater the differences and the fewer the similarities.

EXERCISES

In each exercise write on the dotted line beneath the number the letter *a*, *b*, or *c* of the answer choice which is most like the two drawings at the left. Then on the line above the number give a descriptive name to the things represented by these three drawings. Number one has been worked as an example.

The exercises are graded (put in order) according to increasing difficulty. You should find them easy at first but sooner or later you should reach a point at which your capacity to see abstract similarities must improve for you to continue. The things represented are similar and different according to sensory, affective, and logical qualities in various combinations. Logical similarities and differences, however, predominate, especially at the higher levels of abstraction.

airplanes

1
b

2

3

4

5

6

7

8

9

10

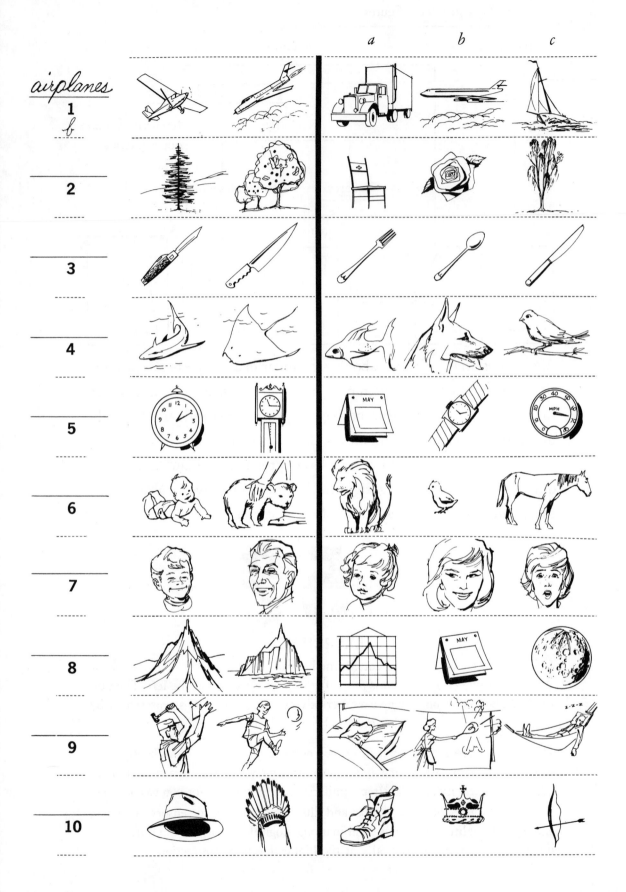

a   b   c

28

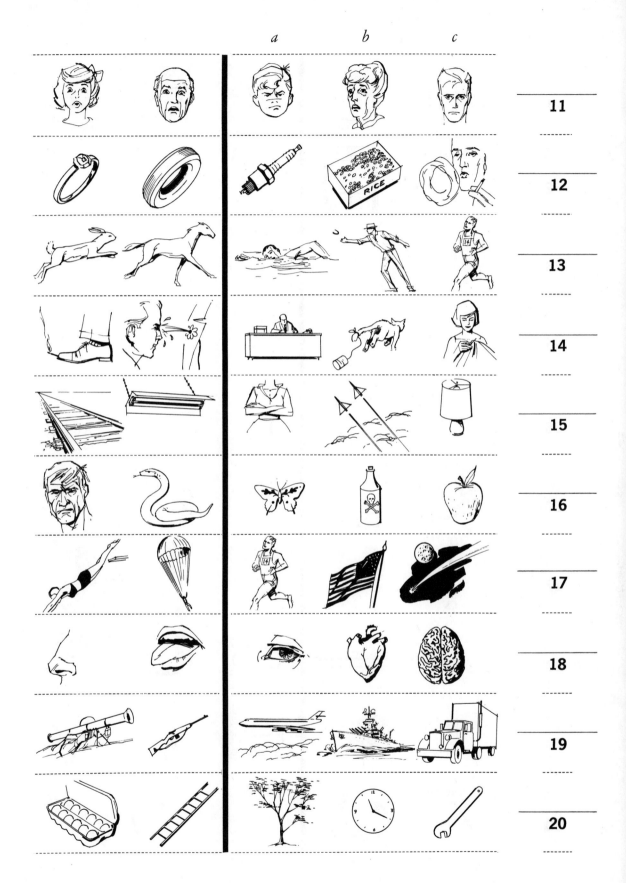

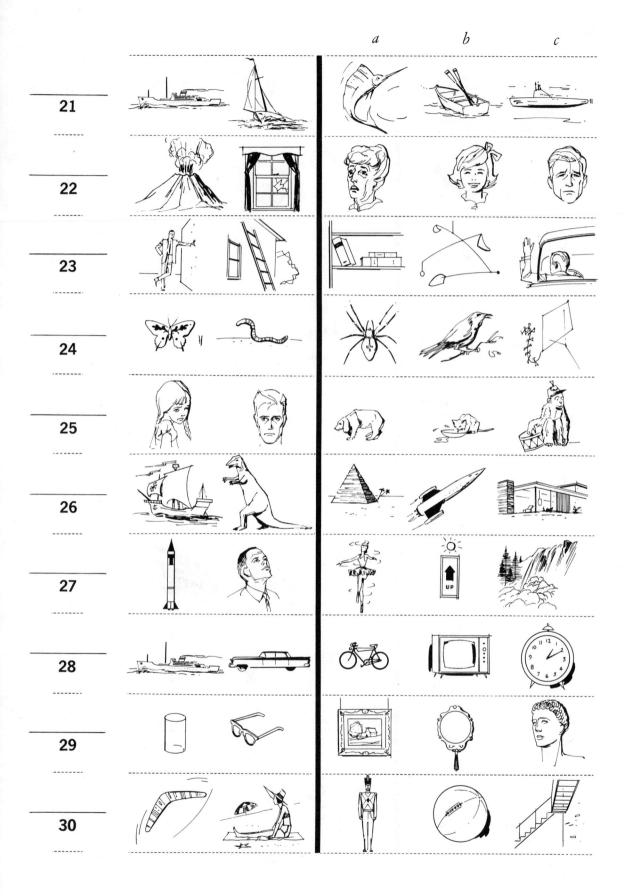

a   b   c

21

22

23

24

25

26

27

28

29

30

30

a   *b*   *c*

31

32

33

34

35

36

37

38

39

40

	a	b	c
41			
42			
43			
44			
45			
46			
47			
48			
49			
50			

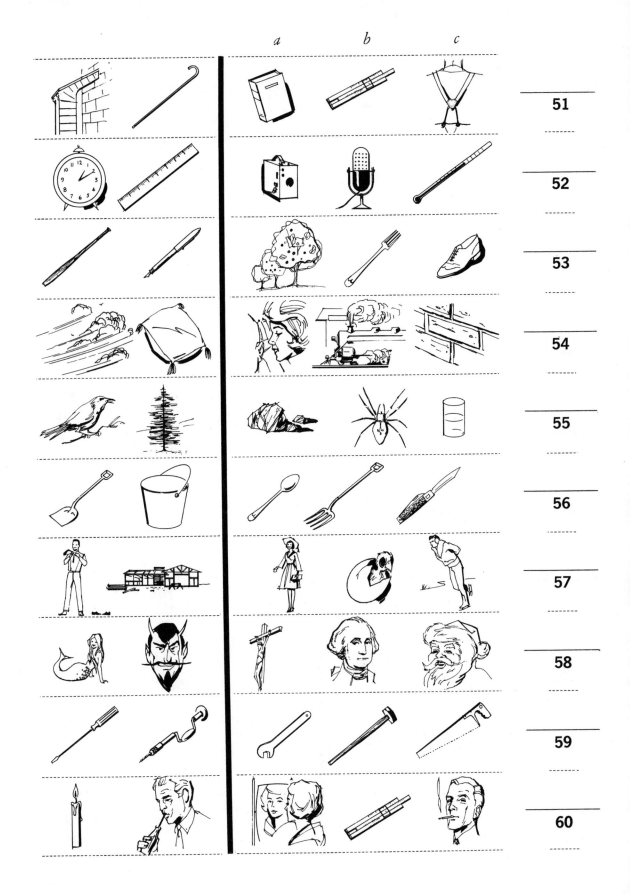

51

52

53

54

55

56

57

58

59

60

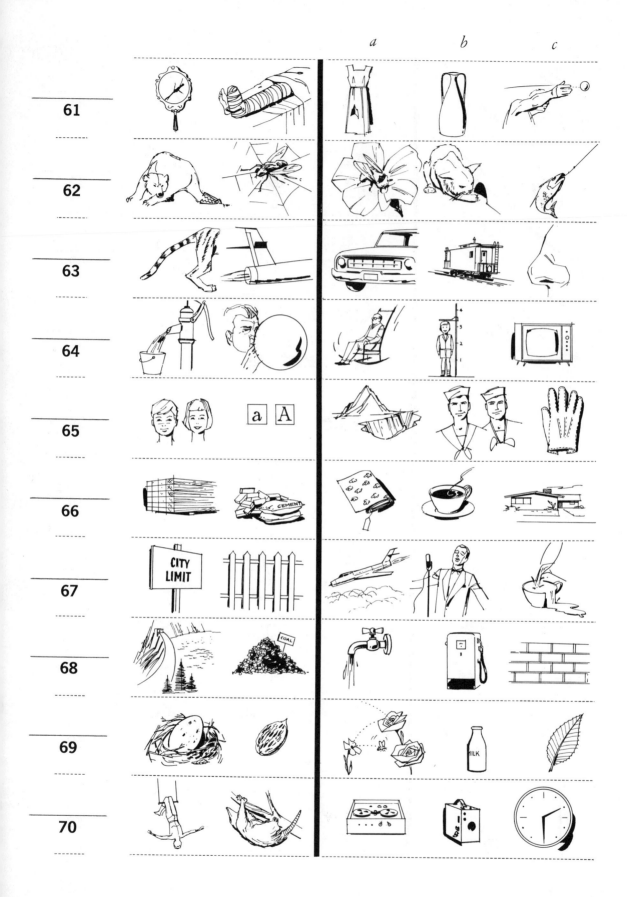

61

62

63

64

65

66

67

68

69

70

a   b   c

34

SIGNS

SECTION 2

2*1

SIGNS, REPRESENTATIONS, AND SYMBOLS

2*1*1

TEXT

Thus far in these exercises in the processes of qualification, we have focused our thinking on the meanings of words and related symbols because qualities are always symbolized conscious responses. And we have emphasized the importance of the sensory-affective-logical classification of qualities. In effect, we have said that you can sort meaningful situations according to modes if there is a dominant quality. Meaningful situations can also be analyzed according to complexity, that is, according to the number of possible meanings a situation may have. When we analyze meaning in this way, we can include kinds of meaning in addition to those derived from words and other symbols.

We pick *sign* as the name for all things that stand for something else. (We must keep in mind, however, that the key words we use in the discussion of mind are always ambiguous and must be defined. A glance at the *sign* entry in the *American Heritage,* the *Random House, Webster's New World,* or *Webster's New Collegiate* dictionary will show you why.) And since the word *ambiguous* is itself ambiguous, we must pause to explain and emphasize what is meant by the *doctrine of essential ambiguity.*

We are told by the Merriam editors that their *Second New International Dictionary* contained over 550,000 entries and that the *Third* contained over 450,000, but they didn't define *entry*. In the *Third*, in the *entry* entry, under *5b3*, we learn that *entry* means "headword" and are asked to "see *vocabulary entry*," where we learn that dictionary entries are usually in boldface type. The entry *boldface* refers us to *blackface*, *sans serif*, and *gothic*, except that *Gothic* meaning "black letter" is also called "Old English." Now we can see that when we say "doctrine of essential ambiguity," we simply mean the idea that a language, to be serviceable, must have a relatively small core of common words with a relatively uncommon number of meanings. From this arises the paradox (ambiguous) that our most familiar (ambiguous) words are the very ones we know least about. In Section 4 we will discuss how these common old words are forever being assigned uncommon new senses that in turn may become *common*—a word that has thirty-seven entries in *Webster's New Collegiate Dictionary*, if we go by the headword rule mentioned above in this commonwealth of ours wherein we the people are all common no matter how uncommon some of us commoners may be. And so by the First Amendment, we have the common right to say that anything that has meaning (ambiguous) is a sign of its meaning. For our purpose we propose three main sorts of sign: simple or natural signs, representations, and symbols.

Simple signs have meanings by necessity; they relate two links in a chain of natural events. Since the sign and its referent have a necessary connection or relationship, the sign must mean the referent or we have misinterpreted it; therefore, simple signs are the least complex—they have the least possible number of meanings. We cannot choose which signs shall stand for which things; we are simply observers of natural occurrences. The red color of the end of a poker is a sign that it is too hot to handle. Red is a quality which, through experience, our minds have associated with heat. We have learned that certain qualities or certain combinations of qualities are signs that a thing is a certain sort of thing. The head of a horse sticking out of a stall is a sign that the body of the horse is within the stall. We know that horse bodies go with horse heads. Thus when we see the head of a horse, under normal circumstances, we also know that it must be connected to the body of a horse, though the body may be hidden from view. The appearance of rain clouds is a sign that rain may fall. One link in a chain of events may indicate that another link is about to follow.

Friday's footprint in the sand was a simple sign to Robinson Crusoe that he was not alone. The footprint was also a representation of the heel-and-sole surface of Friday's foot. *Representations* are signs because they resemble the things they stand for in some way. Although we are no more free to attach any meaning to any representation than we were with simple signs, we can purposely make representations as well as discover them.

Projections are representations that resemble things by means of point-for-point relations. Friday's footprint was a projection—the toe, sole, and heel impressions were spatially related in just the same way that Friday's actual toe, sole, and heel were; the relative depths of the impressions matched the shapes of the actual foot parts as well. The shadow of a tree is a projection because it represents, point for point, a specific object. The shadow is an analogous figure from which we may imaginatively construct the tree, provided we know how the shadow is cast—the position of the sun or other light source. A map is a projection of a certain area of the earth's surface. It is analogous in structure to features of a specific thing for which it stands. A certain line represents a specific highway, another represents the beginning of a specific elevation, another represents a specific county line. In terms of position and distance, the lines on the map are related to each other in the same way as are the elements of the specific terrain the lines represent. We may imaginatively construct the terrain provided we know the *scale* and the *principle of projection* which connect the map meaningfully to the terrain. Though it may not look or sound like its referent, a thing is a projection if it consists of physical elements which are related to each other in the same way as are physical elements of some other specific thing which it represents.

Likenesses are representations that lack the strict point-for-point relation that projections have with their referents. Likenesses may be loose representations of specific things or representations of unspecified members of classes. We may hollow out a "footprint" in wet sand with our fingers that may look like a footprint, but it will bear no point-for-point relationship with any existing foot. If an artist uses a particular horse as a model and is careful to "project" onto his canvas specific "points" of the horse's structure, the painting will be a projection. If it is a freehand sketch of the horse or a drawing of a *horse* without reference to any horse in particular, it is a likeness.

Projections and likenesses can also be thought of as extreme points on a representation continuum. A freehand map of the directions to your home will be more a likeness than a projection if the spatial relationships are inconsistent or if you neglect an important stoplight or highway connection. Paintings and sculptures of actual persons, animals, or landscapes may be placed anywhere on the continuum, depending on their accuracy. Picasso's *Girl in a Mirror* would be a likeness; Andy Warhol's *Marilyn Monroe* would be a projection.

Symbols are different. They are arbitrary, conventional signs that require no resemblance or natural connection whatsoever. They may mean whatever we choose them to mean; therefore, they are the most complex signs, because the possibilities are theoretically infinite. Practically, however, we must agree about what a symbol stands for or it is useless to us. When a child hears a certain sound uttered in connection with a certain thing, he learns to associate the sound with the thing. The sound becomes a stimulus which may by itself produce an impression of the thing in the child's mind. This response is the *meaning* of the sound. Any stimulus may act as a symbol if it is connected *arbitrarily* with a thing. The word *water,* which is a sequence of shapes perceived visually, may stand for the thing water; the sound "freedom" may stand for the thing freedom; a nod, which is a visual gesture, may stand for the recognition of an acquaintance; a handshake, which is primarily a muscular and tactile stimulus, may stand for the feeling of friendship or for the act of agreement. When visual, auditory, or other stimuli are connected arbitrarily with things, they come to *mean* the things.

Symbols may be public or private. Words are public symbols. So are numbers, mathematical symbols, and other marks and things the arbitrary meanings of which are known to more than one individual. A secret mark on an examination paper meaning "unsure of answer" is a private symbol. But even a secret diary must have its secret conventions. Dictionary makers call the symbols we used in the classification examples and exercises in Section 1 (page 3) signs and symbols simply because we are in the habit of referring to some of them as signs. But the marks + or −, for example, are just as symbolic, just as arbitrary and conventional, as the words *plus* or *minus*.

Signs are things that mean something else; simple signs are a matter of natural relationship; representations are a matter of necessary resemblance; and symbols are a matter of conventional association.

EXERCISES

CLASSIFICATION OF SIGNS

The following is a list of signs. In the first blank to the right of each sign, write whether it is a simple sign, a representation, or a symbol. In the second blank write whether the representation is a projection or a likeness, or whether the symbol is public or private. When you have finished, make a classification-analysis diagram of these signs and include horizontal sorting factors.

	Main Sort	*Subsort*
1. VII	_____	_____
2. *Alaska,* as, "Alaska is our largest state."	_____	_____
3. The shadow of a building	_____	_____
4. *In,* as, "George is in real estate."	_____	_____
5. A blinking turn signal on a car	_____	_____
6. *X,* as in the formula, $X - Y = Z$	_____	_____
7. 138	_____	_____
8. *Red,* as, "His shirt is red."	_____	
9. The trunk and limbs of a tree, meaning there are roots beneath the ground	_____	_____
10. A map of Germany	_____	_____
11. =, as in the formula, $X - 17 = 24$	_____	_____
12. A piece of string tied to a finger, meaning remember to send Aunt Bertha a thank-you note.	_____	_____
13. A rain cloud, meaning rain may fall	_____	_____
14. The music from a phonograph record, representing the original music which produced the record	_____	_____
15. A motion picture cartoon	_____	_____
16. A cough, indicating that someone has a cold	_____	_____
17. The Big Dipper	_____	_____
18. The springy feel of a pillow, meaning it is made of foam rubber	_____	_____

2*122

IDENTIFICATION OF SIGNS

In the blank space of each sentence below indicate whether the sign is a *simple sign, projection, likeness,* or *symbol.*

1. A hoarse cough is a _____ of a cold.
2. A man's fingerprint at the scene of a crime is a _____ that he was present.
3. A drawing of a man (no man in particular) is a _____.
4. A cross is a _____ of Christianity.
5. A fingerprint is a _____ of the surface of the finger which made it.
6. The flag of the United States is a _____ of the United States.
7. A clever remark is a _____ of intelligence.
8. A brand on a steer is a _____ of the end of a branding iron.
9. A brand on a steer is a _____ of the steer's ownership.
10. A woman's reflection in a mirror is a _____ of the woman.
11. A blush is a _____ of shyness.
12. A wrinkled brow is a _____ of concentration.
13. A horrified expression is a _____ of fear.
14. A statement is a _____ of its meaning.
15. Large muscles are a _____ of a person's strength.
16. A statue of George Washington is a _____ of him.
17. A rain cloud is a _____ of rain.
18. Auditory impulses are a _____ of the sound waves which produce them.
19. A red traffic light is a _____ to stop.
20. A stain is a _____ that something has been spilled.
21. A white flag on a battlefield is a _____ of surrender.
22. Placing the index finger vertically before the lips is a _____ to be quiet.
23. A wave is a _____ of greeting.
24. A visual image on the retina of the eye is a _____ of the scene which it represents.
25. The retreat of the enemy's troops is a _____ of victory.
26. An Indian smoke signal is a _____.
27. A stain is a _____ of an area of spilled fluid.
28. Fluent speech is a _____ of an agile mind.
29. A skid mark is a _____ that a car has skidded.
30. A very realistic portrait is a _____ of a person.
31. The man in the moon is a _____.

32. A policeman's badge is a _____ of his authority.

33. A sergeant's stripes are a _____ of his rank.

34. A blinking turn signal on the right side of a car is a _____ of the driver's intention to turn right.

35. A clenched fist is a _____ of anger.

36. A rainbow is sometimes considered a _____ of happiness.

37. A bathtub ring is a _____ of the level of the water previously contained in the tub.

38. The annual rings of a tree are a _____ of the tree's age.

39. Erect posture may be a _____ of pride.

40. Caution is often a _____ of prudence.

41. A skid mark is a _____ of the path of a skidding car.

42. A cartoon drawing of a talking animal is a _____ of an imaginary creature.

43. A signal for troops to begin firing is a _____.

44. A word in Morse code is a _____.

45. A bear track is a _____ of the presence of a bear.

46. An ambulance siren is a _____ for motorists to pull off the road.

47. ⋈ is a _____ of a mirage.

48. In astronomy ☉ is a _____ of the sun.

49. High blood pressure is often a _____ of circulatory disorder.

50. A bear track is a _____ of the bear's paw.

51. Inflammation is often a _____ of infection.

52. Spurting blood is a _____ that an artery rather than a vein has been cut.

53. In astronomy ☄ is a _____ of a comet.

54. A death mask is a _____ of a dead man's face.

55. In astronomy ♀ is a _____ of Venus.

56. In biology and botany ♀ is a _____ that an organism, cell, or organ is female.

57. A racing pulse is a _____ of excitement.

58. A plastic toy is a _____ of the mould which formed it.

59. A plastic toy representing a dog is a _____.

60. The words on a page of a book are a _____ of a plate of type on a printing press.

61. Low barometric pressure is a _____ of rain.

62. The firmness of a head of lettuce is a _____ of its quality.

63. Modesty is often a _____ of virtue.

64. A drawing of Mickey Mouse is a _____ of a mouse.

65. The brand name of a product is often a _____ of its quality.

66. Stimulation of the visual area of the brain is a _____ of an image on the retina of the eye.

67. % is a _____ of percent (as, 10%).

68. A good credit record is a _____ that a man can be trusted to pay a debt.

69. In chemistry H_2O is a _____ of water.

70. In electricity R or r is a _____ of resistance.

71. A motion picture is a _____ of the changing frames of a motion picture reel.

72. A mirage is a _____ of a distant scene.

73. A photographic print is a _____ of a negative.

74. Pain is usually a _____ of physical disorder.

75. In electricity —⋀⋀— is a _____ of a resistor.

76. A chart is a _____ of a region of water.

77. Lack of energy may be a _____ of vitamin deficiency.

78. Rough hands may be a _____ that a man is a laborer.

79. On a highway ⤴ is a _____ of a right curve.

80. A scale model is a _____ of an actual object.

81. In mathematics π is a _____ of pi, the number 3.141592+, which is obtained by dividing the circumference of a circle by the diameter.

82. A drawing of Dick Tracy is a _____ of a man.

83. In mathematics ∴ is a _____ meaning "therefore."

84. A hearty appetite is a _____ of health.

85. Tears are usually a _____ of sorrow.

86. The setting sun is a _____ of the coming of night.

87. Excessive crime is a _____ of a decadent society.

88. Lengthening shadows are a _____ that day is ending.

89. $ is a _____ that a number refers to dollars.

90. A clear reflection is a _____ of a placid lake.

91. In music ♪ is a _____ of an eighth note.

92. A television program is a _____ of certain of the visual and auditory aspects of a performance in a television studio.

93. Apples are a _____ that a tree is an apple tree.

94. ⌒ is a _____ of a rainbow.

95. A dress is a _____ that the wearer is female.

96. A mental image is often a _____ of some remembered object.

97. To a postal clerk an airmail stamp is a _____ that a letter should be sent by air.

98. The outside (visible portion) of a cherry is a _____ that there is a pit inside.

99. A picture of a balance is a _____ of justice.

100. A shadow dance is a _____ of unseen performers.

2*1*2*3

DISCOVERY AND CREATION OF SIGNS

On a separate sheet of paper perform the operations indicated in each exercise.

SIGNS (SIMPLE)

1. Name three signs of Spring.
2. Name three signs of fatigue.
3. Name three signs that a store has been robbed.
4. Name three signs that a man is a doctor.
5. Name three signs that someone is unhappy.
6. Name three signs that a restaurant is closed for the night.
7. Name three signs that a country is at war.
8. Name three signs that an automobile radiator is overheated.
9. Name three signs that a person is telling a lie.
10. Name three signs that a person is a hypochondriac.
11. Name three signs that a person is intelligent.
12. Name three signs that an animal is a cow.
13. Name three signs that a certain candidate will win an election.
14. Name three signs of death.
15. List a number of signs of some occurrence, condition, or other thing of interest to you.
16. Name two or three signs which others may have perceived in your behavior recently. That is, name statements, facial expressions, or other elements of your actions which may have given other people information about you.

LIKENESSES

17. Draw from memory a caricature of the face of someone you know. Then consider in what ways the drawing is a likeness and in what ways it is a projection.
18. Make a three-dimensional likeness of some object, such as a person, animal, house, or automobile. Use any appropriate material, such as clay, wood, or a cake of soap.
19. Draw or paint an abstract picture which is a likeness of a thing or scene only in certain general respects. Stress the differences rather than the similarities but make sure that *some* elements of similarity are present.
20. Make a likeness of a face, using toothpicks, matches, paper clips, or other small objects.
21. Give three examples of auditory likenesses — that is, likenesses which are perceived by hearing. Be careful *not* to list auditory projections.
22. Can you draw a likeness which can represent more than one thing? Are there such things as ambiguous likenesses?

PROJECTIONS

23. Name five ways of making a projection of one of your hands or its outline.
24. Name two ways of making on a flat surface a projection of the surface of a

sphere, such as the earth. It may be helpful to look up in your dictionary the terms *orthographic projection, oblique projection, trimetric projection, conic projection, cylindrical projection, gnomic projection, Mercator's projection,* and *stereographic projection.*

25. Can the eye see itself by other means than reflection?

26. Can you think of a projection which may be perceived by a sense other than hearing or vision?

SYMBOLS

27. List two symbols which may stand for the object pictured below.

28. Give two symbols which may stand for the number of days in a week.

29. Name a historical personage that might be thought of as a symbol of courage.

30. Invent a gesture, other than a wave, signifying farewell.

31. How would you go about symbolizing the boundaries of a piece of property you own?

32. The average velocity of an object may be defined as the average distance traveled by the object in a unit of time, such as an hour, minute, or second. If a car travels 100 miles in two hours, its average velocity is 50 miles an hour. Express this relationship in a formula consisting of symbols of your own choosing.

33. The average or mean age of four men aged 20, 30, 40, and 50 is 35. The average deviation of the ages of the men from the mean age is ten years. This value is obtained by dividing the sum of the individual deviations from the mean by the number of ages. Using symbols of your own choosing, write a formula for determining the average deviation from the mean of any group of numbers.

34. Below is an alphabetical list of the members of a service club. Norris and Talbot are inactive members, who are not required to pay dues. Alsop, Martin, and Farley are two months behind in their dues. Parker and Smith are a month behind. The rest are up to date. Signify this information by making a mark by each name below. Then ask yourself whether your marks are public or private symbols.

ALLEN	HARDING	PARKER
ALSOP	MARTIN	ROBERTS
CORNING	NORRIS	SMITH
FARLEY	OGDEN	TALBOT

35. In an imaginary language ✳ ⊙ means "old man," ⊕ ☐ means "old woman," and ✳ ⊠ means "hungry man." If ⊕ means "woman," what is a synonym for ⊙ ?

36. Invent a code or other symbol system capable of expressing a simple statement, such as, "Give me liberty or give me death."

SYMBOLS

AMBIGUITY

TEXT

Because any stimulus may be associated with any thing, all symbols are potentially ambiguous — that is, capable of having two or more senses. And most of our commonly-used symbols *are* ambiguous. The word *stern* may mean "the rear end of a sailing vessel" (as, The captain walked to the stern); or "strict" (as, Her parents are stern). The word *sound* may mean "auditory sensation, noise" (as, Do you like the sound of rain?); "the vibrations in air causing auditory sensation" (as, Light travels much faster than sound); "to make a sound" (as, Sound the alarm); "in good health" (as, The doctor found him sound); "trustworthy, reliable" (as, Lawyers generally give sound advice); "channel or strait" (as, The ship was anchored in the sound); "to fathom" (as, They sounded the channel); or "to dive" (as, The whale sounded). A plus sign may mean "added to" (as, $5 + 9 = 14$); "slightly greater than" (as, $9.3+$); "positive, not negative," said of numbers (as, $+2$); "positive," said of charged particles having more protons than electrons; "in combination with" (as, $2H_2 + O_2 \rightarrow 2H_2O$); or "a partial grade higher than" (as, She got a B+ in Algebra). The symbol ∞ may mean "infinity" in the field of mathematics, "of an indefinite number," as of stamens, in the field of biology, or "haze" in the field of weather reporting. The symbol X may mean "ten" when used as a Roman numeral; "the signature of a man who cannot write"; "the element xenon"; "an unknown quantity" (as, Let X equal...); "multiplied by"; or "abscissa." Many of our verbal symbols, such as *turn, line, point, light, make,* and *head,* have more than fifty recorded senses. The word *set* has over two hundred. Extreme ambiguity is a characteristic of the symbols we use most often. All symbols are potentially, if not actually, ambiguous.

The knowledge that symbols may have several senses tends to streamline the operation of communication. If an interpreter knows that *horse* may mean "sawhorse" as well as "animal with four legs and mane," he is likely to understand an utterer when he says, "My horse has a splintered leg." One should treat the symbols of others as the ambiguities that they are and select from among the various possible meanings of each the one which best fits the circumstances. When using symbols himself he should take care to define for himself and others the range of meaning which he wishes each symbol to designate. In a communication situation the utterer and the interpreter should cooperate to make sure they are connecting the same symbols with the same things.

2*21*2

EXERCISES

1. List five words which you believe to be unambiguous. Then look them up in your dictionary. _____, _____, _____, _____, _____
2. What one word may stand; in different contexts, for each of the following: an adult, male human being; a human being; the human race; a valet; and a game piece, as in chess? _____
3. List five senses of the word *order*.

   A_____

   B_____

C_____

D_____

E_____

4. In the space before each sentence write the letter of the definition which corresponds to the use of *ring* in that sentence.

A _____ She wore a small *ring* on her finger.

a. Sound of a bell

B _____ Did you *ring* the chimes?

b. Site of a boxing match

C _____ Do you see that *ring* of trees?

c. To circle

D _____ The clown was performing in the *ring*.

d. To cause a resonant body to sound

E _____ The boxer left the *ring*.

e. Circular band worn on the finger

F _____ I'll give you a *ring* sometime.

f. A number of people working together for a common, selfish end

G _____ The pilot banked his plane and began to *ring* the field.

g. An enclosed, usually circular area for circus exhibitions

H _____ He tried to *ring* the bottle.

h. Telephone call

I _____ He tried to *ring* the donkey.

i. To call by telephone

J _____ The *ring* of gangsters was broken up by the police.

j. A number of objects grouped in a circle

K _____ I was going to *ring* you but I forgot your number.

k. To put a ring in the nose of

L _____ I heard a loud *ring*.

l. To toss a ring over

5. In the space before each sentence at the left write the letter of the sentence at the right which contains the same sense of the word *watch*.

A _____ *Watch* that your wits don't fail you.

a. Didn't you *watch* the want ads for a job?

B _____ Aren't you going to *watch* the parade?

b. The children want to *watch* the plumber fix the sink.

C _____ His *watch* keeps good time.

c. His relief came before the end of his *watch*.

D _____ One should *watch* for a chance to improve himself.

d. *Watch* that you don't paint yourself into a corner.

E _____ The sentinel had a quiet *watch*.

e. She left her *watch* at the jeweler's.

6. To the right of each sentence below compose another sentence using the word *bank* in the same sense.

A _____ The *bank* is closed.

a. _____

_____

B _____ He paddled toward the *bank*.

b. _____

_____

50

C ____ She skied into a *bank*
of snow.

c. _____
_____

D ____ The *bank* of lights came on
when he replaced the fuse.

d. _____
_____

E ____ A pilot should *bank* his
plane when making a turn.

e. _____
_____

7. Count the number of senses per word, or entry, on one of the pages of your dictionary. _____

8. Pick at random a sentence from a newspaper or magazine and determine the average number of senses per word by looking up each in your dictionary. _____

9. As in problem eight determine the average number of senses per word of a sentence chosen from a textbook or other volume which you consider difficult to read. _____

10. Count the number of senses listed for the word *set* in an abridged dictionary, in an unabridged dictionary, and in the *Oxford English Dictionary,* if it is available in your library.

_____, _____, _____

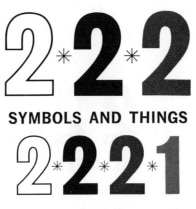

SYMBOLS AND THINGS

TEXT

In order for an utterer or an interpreter to deal with symbols as ambiguities, he must know how to distinguish symbols from things. He must know when he, or another, is speaking of a symbol and when he, or another, is speaking of a thing by means of a symbol. If a man says, "What does *moon* mean?" he is speaking of a symbol. But if he says, "What is the moon?" he is speaking of a thing by means of a symbol. The word *moon* may mean "the natural satellite of the earth," "any natural planetary satellite," "any natural or artificial planetary satellite," "moonlight," or "to go about as if moonstruck." Let us imagine that an utterer says, "By *moon* I mean any natural satellite of a planet. Deimos, for example, is a moon of Mars," and that an interpreter replies, "No, no. That isn't the moon. The moon has craters and goes around the earth." In this instance communication fails to take place because of ignorance in the interpreter's mind of the distinction between a symbol and a thing. The interpreter may be thinking of *the* moon while the utterer is referring to a sense which the word *moon* may have.

The confusion between symbols and things is common when symbols are used in abstract senses. In using the word *intelligence* an utterer may mean "the score of an individual on an IQ test." But an interpreter may think he is referring to the thing intelligence (one of the things to which *intelligence* may refer) rather than defining the word. Thus he may feel that the utterer's "definition" of "intelligence," the "thing," is inaccurate since IQ scores are not necessarily valid measures of "intelligence." The interpreter will continue to misunderstand the utterer until he sees that he is not defining a thing but defining a word, which he is using to refer, in this case, to a thing other than "the" thing. Symbols may be used to refer to things or to the "things" (symbols) which stand for them. A knowledge of the distinction between these two operations is essential to accurate communication.

EXERCISES

In each exercise write in the boxes in the middle of the page two words which may stand for the things indicated in the box at the left. Then in the boxes at the right indicate for each word two *other* things which it may signify.

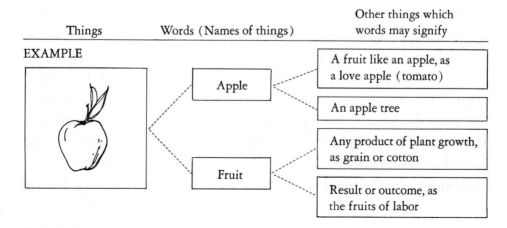

Things	Words (Names of things)	Other things which words may signify
EXAMPLE	Apple	A fruit like an apple, as a love apple (tomato)
		An apple tree
	Fruit	Any product of plant growth, as grain or cotton
		Result or outcome, as the fruits of labor

1

2

3

4

5

53

2*2*3

SYMBOLS AND THEIR MATRICES

2*23*1

TEXT

In order for an ambiguous symbol to be used in a specific sense, it must be placed in a matrix. A matrix is everything in the universe except the symbol itself. An important element of a matrix is the context, the other symbols surrounding the symbol in question. The words *A...is a citrus fruit* make up the context of *lime* in the sentence, "A lime is a citrus fruit." The matrix of *lime* consists of its context together with the identity of the utterer, the time and place of the utterance, and everything else in the universe, including the moon, stars, and galaxies. One of the possible senses of a symbol becomes the likely interpretation when the symbol is placed in a matrix. When the word *lime* is placed in a matrix involving chemical substances, the likely interpretation of the word is "calcium oxide" rather than "citrus fruit." When an ambiguous symbol is placed in a context of other ambiguous symbols, the environmental signs of the matrix together with the pattern of possible senses of the symbols of the context produce a system of relationships in the interpreter's mind. The interpreter then picks a sense of the symbol which has a meaningful relationship to the probable senses of the other symbols and to the environment of the utterance, the setting in which the symbols were spoken or written. Other possible senses of the symbol are thus eliminated. The effect of placing a symbol in a matrix is the indication of a specific sense of the symbol.

Not all of the elements of a matrix need be relevant to the interpretation of a symbol. We need not refer to the galaxy in Andromeda in order to interpret *hill* in "Jack and Jill went up the hill..." But in the interpretation of almost every symbol some elements of the matrix other than the context need to be considered. A knowledge of the time of the utterance is often necessary. An eighteenth century use of the word *jet* might signify a stream of water or a black mineral substance, but not a jet aircraft or the stream of gases produced by its engine. The place of an utterance may also be an important sign of the meaning of a symbol. If an American uses the word *tea* he may mean simply a hot drink somewhat like coffee, but in the matrix of British society *tea* may mean a late afternoon repast in which tea is served. One must be aware of both the time and the place of Shakespeare's matrix in order to discover that the word *lime* in *Hamlet* may mean birdlime, a sticky substance spread on twigs to catch birds. In order to comprehend the meaning of a symbol, an interpreter must consider relevant aspects of the symbol's matrix, however unaware he may be that he is performing the operation.

2*2*3*2

EXERCISES

1. Five words are listed below together with two senses for each. On a separate sheet of paper place each word into a context appropriate to each sense listed. Then for each use of the word describe additional elements of a matrix which might surround it.

EXAMPLE

Word	Senses	Contexts	Additional elements of matrices
heal:	a. To close, forming a scar	How long will it take the wound to heal?	This statement might have been made by a patient in a doctor's office.
	b. To remedy a mental condition	Cynthia tried to heal the wounds which her harsh words had inflicted on Gregory.	This might have been said on a TV soap opera in the 1960's in the USA.

A. *point:*   a. A score or unit of a score, as in athletic games. b. To hold and aim an object toward something.

B. *drive:*   a. A mechanism which transfers motion from one part of a machine to another. b. A ride in a car.

C. *bent:*   a. Angular; crooked; not straight. b. An inclination or tendency; determined state.

D. *nucleus:*   a. The inner part of an atom. b. The central or fundamental element of anything.

E. *take:*   a. To subject oneself to something without active resistance. b. To eat or otherwise consume.

2. Indicate three possible matrices for each sentence below.

A. He lost his man.
B. What state is she in?
C. He took the pass to the front.
D. He saw her through the plant.
E. She heard a dog whistle.
F. I'll see you.

G. Is she religious?
H. Don't they set well?
I. The service was poor.
J. The issue is suspect.
K. Those models are finished.
L. She was innocent.

3. Place each of the following words into five different contexts. Then indicate additional elements of a matrix for each use.

A. band
B. atmosphere
C. auxiliary
D. stock
E. range

F. function
G. light
H. respect
I. rest
J. sense

4. Each of the following words is used frequently today and was also common to English speakers in previous centuries, but with a different meaning. Place

each word in an earlier context and in a current context and list both meanings. The *Oxford English Dictionary* will be a useful resource.

A. go   F. villain
B. eager   G. minister
C. undertaker   H. silly
D. deer   I. dope
E. girl   J. bureau

*   *   *   *   *

ANALYSIS

SECTION 3

INTRODUCTION TO ANALYSIS

TEXT

In order to get down to the main business of this book, it was necessary to explore the basic concepts from which it derived. These are three: the concept of symbols as human artifacts, the concept of meaning gained from quality or signs, and the concept of essential ambiguity. We introduced the classification process first because the genus-species relation is the foundation of all logical analysis. Although we began with classification in the study of analysis, we would emphasize the fact that the part-whole relation and the stage-operation relation similarly give rise to the processes we call structure analysis and operation analysis. Symbols —particularly language symbols—are the primary instruments of all three analytical processes which produce the systems of law, order, and science we call civilization.

Although symbols are the primary instruments of all three forms of analysis, the focus of each form is fundamentally different and therefore the questions we must ask and answer are different. You know that when we classify, we answer the questions What is this a *sort* of? and What are the *sorts* of this? On the other hand, when we perform a structure analysis, we answer the questions What is this a *part* of? and What are the *parts* of this? And when we perform an operation analysis, we answer the questions What is this a *stage* of? and What are the *stages* of this? When we say, "A man is a kind of animal," we are classifying. When we say, "A leg is part of a man," we are performing a structure analysis. When we say, "Childhood is a stage in a man's life," we are performing an operation analysis. Classification has to do with *kinds* of things. Structure analysis has to do with *parts* of things. Operation analysis has to do with *stages of change* in things.

3*1*12

EXERCISES

The exercises below will give you practice in distinguishing among the three sorts of analysis. Write the number of each item in the appropriate pigeonhole. The number of the first item has already been correctly placed.

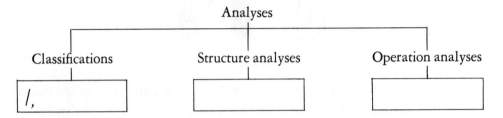

Analyses

Classifications | Structure analyses | Operation analyses

1,

1. Organisms
   Animals
      Men
      Animals
   Plants

2. Tree
      Trunk
      Limbs
      Roots

3. Morning
      Getting up
      Eating breakfast
      Going to work
   Afternoon
   Evening

4.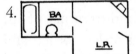

5. Men
      Good
      Bad

6.

7. Man
   Head
   Trunk
   Limbs

8. 1961
      January
      February
      Other months
   1962
      January
      February
      Other months

9. Substances
      Solids
         Metals
         Nonmetals
      Liquids
      Gases

10. Nourishment
      Eating
         Chewing
         Swallowing
      Digestion
      Elimination

11. America
      California
         Los Angeles County
         San Bernardino County
      Oregon
      Other states

12. The ax had a long wooden handle and an iron head with a razor-sharp blade.

13. John and George are servicemen. John is a sailor; George, a soldier.

14. After finishing the housework Mrs. Jones did her shopping. First she went to the bakery, where she bought two loaves of bread. She then went to the grocery store.

15. The courthouse is two blocks south of Fourth Street on the east side of Orange Avenue.

16. While all people are either acquaintances or strangers, not all acquaintances are friends.

17. After winning the war for independence the people allowed a temporary dictatorship to be established by the leader of the revolution, who justified his actions on grounds of expediency.

CLASSIFICATION

TEXT

DEFINITIONS

The process of classification is aided by the use of these terms: *genus, species, specimen, quality, vertical sorting factor,* and *horizontal sorting factor.* You have already worked with most of these terms, but the following extended definitions and examples will serve both as a review and as an aid in making more complex analyses.

As we use them, *genus* and *species* are logical rather than biological terms. A genus term is simply the name of a class, and species terms are the names of the two or more subclasses the genus includes. You will note that in our diagrams all genus and species terms go with vertical lines, which always imply that the items below are similar. The horizontal lines stand for the respect in which the two or more species differ under any one vertical factor. As you work down a branch of a diagram, the upper term is always a genus term and the attached lower terms are species. Thus the name of a "pigeonhole" is a genus in relation to the "pigeons," but we have found it desirable to call it a species and an individual pigeon a *specimen* because a particular pigeon is even more special than the rest of the pigeons in the same hole. Of course all specimens differ from one another, but not for us as long as they are in the same pigeonhole; once we differentiate among them we must draw the line of the horizontal sorting factor and add a new set of vertical sorting factors and pigeonholes. For example, the qualities which are common to all books prompt the use of the genus term *book*. The qualities which are common only to certain species of books prompt the use of such terms as *novel* and *historical novel*. The qualities which are peculiar to a single specimen of books prompt the use of a proper name, such as *my copy of Gone With the Wind*. If we only want to arrange our books according to their general format—novel, biography, reference, and so forth—then our copies of *Gone With the Wind* and *Doctor Zhivago* will share the same pigeonhole. However, if we sort further into countries of origin or whether they are translations, then they will not. Since each specimen is unique (even two copies of *Dr. Zhivago* may differ in edition, size, condition, and so forth), each could ultimately occupy a single pigeonhole, if our purpose dictates it. For example, if our purpose is to arrange our library according to genre, then a classification of books by Jessamyn West will occupy several pigeonholes and each hole will often contain several pigeons, as the following diagram illustrates:

Books* by Jessamyn West

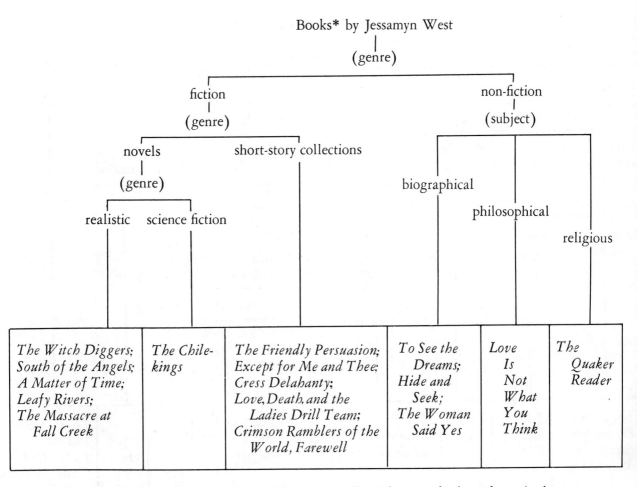

* For this problem, *books* is defined as independent works bound as single volumes.

But if we are preparing a paper on Miss West's books of fiction and the possible parallels with her life, we will note more extensive similarities and differences among the books, and the pigeonholes will most often contain a single item, as this diagram illustrates:

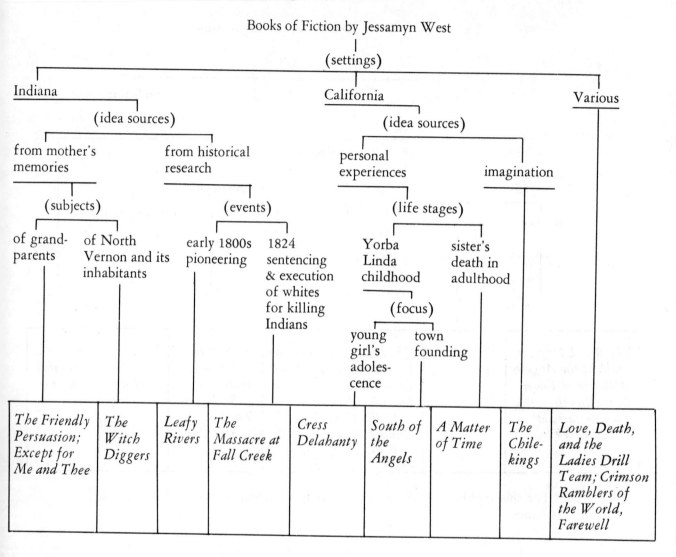

In working down a branch level by level in what we call a *working classification,* we multiply and record relevant qualities by means of our horizontal sorting factors. The result is tantamount to a systematic definition of the problem in hand; indeed *systematics,* like *taxonomy,* has been a synonym for classification throughout the history of modern science. We might say that classification is the first stage in the development of a complete science and the one in which the essential function of symbol systems is most obvious.

3*2·1*2

SORTS OF CLASSIFICATIONS

There are two sorts of classifications: classifications of collected specimens and classifications of specimens to be collected. When a man rearranges the books in his home, he is classifying collected specimens; when a bookstore owner makes a tentative list of books to order, he is classifying specimens to be collected. A classification of specimens to be collected may be called a working classification. When an individual makes a working classification he decides what sorts of things to obtain for later analysis. Once the specimens are collected a working classification may be replaced, in many cases, by a classification of collected specimens. A working classification is a means of deciding what sorts of things to obtain; a classification of collected specimens is a means of sorting things which have already been obtained.

The distinction between the two sorts of classifications is vital. It is as foolish to collect specimens without a working classification as it is to build a house without a plan. Working classifications are plans just as analyses of planned structures and planned operations are plans. Working classifications determine future action as do structural and operational plans. A working classification of building materials may help an architect decide what a house should be made of, just as a floor plan and other drawings determine what the structure of the house shall be and a building schedule determines the manner in which the house shall be built. Working classifications are plans of sorts of things, whether objects or information, to collect.

Let us examine in further detail the distinction between the process of working classification and the process of classifying collected specimens. If we make a list of groceries before going to the market, we may find that our "working classification" has empty "pigeonholes" once the "specimens" have been collected. The market may be out of baking powder, for example. But if we classify the groceries once they have been bought, all the "pigeonholes" of the diagram will be filled. Baking powder, being absent, simply will not be included in the classification diagram. A working classification is often a statement of intention; it indicates possibilities which may not occur to us if we limit our attention merely to that which is present.

Let us imagine that two writers are preparing articles about the causes of automobile accidents. One proceeds to collect data with the aid of a working classification; the other proceeds intuitively, with the idea that he will organize the data once he has gathered them. The first writer decides that within a certain field of information, such as current newspapers and magazines, he will make a notation of all reports of automobile accidents. This approach allows him to be objective in his information gathering. The second writer has the idea that more accidents are caused by women than by men; consequently he tends to read articles dealing with accidents caused by women. As a result the data which he collects are weighted in the direction of his original prejudice. The working classification of the first writer may appear as follows:

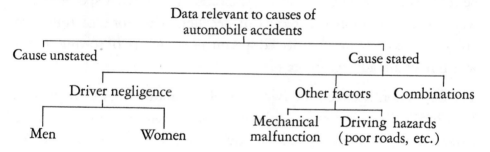

The second writer's classification of collected data may appear as follows, though he may not use this form of notation:

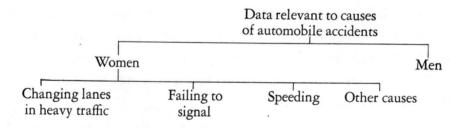

The second writer may collect data only from articles where the human cause of the accident is stated, and his prejudice together with his lack of an objective approach may cause him within this narrow range to collect more data relevant to accidents caused by women than by men. By considering in advance all the possible sorts of information, the first writer enables himself to collect not only data relevant to accidents caused by driver negligence but also data relevant to accidents caused by other factors, such as faulty steering wheels and wet pavement. He may even take note of articles in which the cause of the accident is unstated. The first writer may be prejudiced against women drivers, too, but his objective approach to the problem enables him to discover the truth rather than to reinforce a possibly false belief. The "research" of the second writer may lead him to write an article entitled, "Why Women Are a Driving Menace." The research of the first writer may lead him to conclude that women cause more accidents than men but that the accidents caused by men are more serious. He may discover, on the other hand, that men have more accidents due to driving negligence but that women have more accidents due to mechanical malfunction, which may be the result of another kind of negligence. He may discover that in most reports of accidents the cause is unstated and that a valid conclusion therefore cannot be reached, or he may find evidence that male reporters in their news articles tend to play up accidents caused by women and that consequently the journalistic sources of information about traffic accidents may not provide an accurate picture of the facts. An article by the first writer might be entitled, "Are Men Reporters Fair to Women Drivers?" By the use of a working classification, the first writer has a better chance of discovering the facts concerning the causes of traffic accidents and writing a truthful article. The second writer is likely to fool himself as well as his readers. A working classification is a device which embodies a procedure leading to a result consistent with one's intention. It is a plan which enables a person to gather information or objects relevant to his purpose.

Although we have suggested that working classifications may be replaced with classifications of collected specimens, often a fusion of the two is the most useful. That is, by keeping the vertical sorting factors of the working classification in our classification of collected specimens, even when no specimens are found, we maintain the objectivity and completeness of the original research. It is clear evidence that the data were searched for, not that they were simply overlooked. Thus, empty pigeonholes can reveal important facts. For example, the first writer may be doing research in a community for an auto insurance company, and the ages of the men and women may be as relevant as their sex in figuring their accident potential (and therefore their annual premiums). The researcher may find that no accidents were caused by women aged thirty to forty in that community during the specified time span. Thus the empty pigeonhole for the female-aged-thirty-to-forty vertical sorting factor would be highly significant and a fact that would influence insurance rates.

3*21*3

METHOD OF CLASSIFICATION

The following stages are a summary of the classification procedure discussed in Section 1:

I. NAME THE SPECIMENS
II. CHOOSE APPROPRIATE HORIZONTAL AND VERTICAL
    SORTING FACTORS
III. DIVIDE SPECIMENS INTO CATEGORIES
    A. MAIN CATEGORIES
    B. SUBCATEGORIES
    OTHERS

If our purpose in sorting fruits is to make a table display, *color, shape, texture,* and *beauty* may be appropriate horizontal sorting factors. Our vertical sorting factors may be words such as *red* and *luscious.* If we are sorting fruits for the purpose of eating them, *taste, vitamins, calories,* and *proteins* may be appropriate horizontal sorting factors, and appropriate vertical sorting factors may be terms such as *sour, tart, high in vitamin C,* and *low in calories. Taste, vitamins, calories,* and *proteins* would be irrelevant to a table-display purpose, as would *color, shape, texture,* and *beauty* be secondary or irrelevant to an eating purpose. By listing as many possible horizontal sorting factors as we can think of to begin with, we enable ourselves to decide which factors are relevant and which are irrelevant to our purpose.

The division of specimens, collected or to be collected, into categories goes hand in hand with the choice of sorting factors. We may treat this act of division, however, as a separate process which may itself be divided into stages. The first stage involves the division of the specimens into main categories. The second stage involves the division of the main categories into subcategories. The third and succeeding stages involve continued acts of division. Because the mind operates best with small numbers of items, the specimens to be classified should, in most cases, be divided into no more than six or seven main categories, and a main category should be divided into no more than six or seven subcategories.

3*22*

TEXT-RELATED EXERCISES

1. Answer the following questions by referring to the diagram below.

```
                    Animals
         ┌─────────────┼──────────────┐
     Land animals          Fish           Birds
    ┌──────┴──────┐
 Humans         Animals
```

A. What are two species of land animals? _____,
   _____

B. What are three species of animals? _____, _____,
   _____

C. What is the genus of the species fish? _____

D. What is the genus of the species humans? _____

E. Look up *genus* and *species* in your dictionary. How are these terms used
   in biology?

2. Answer the following questions by referring to the diagram below.

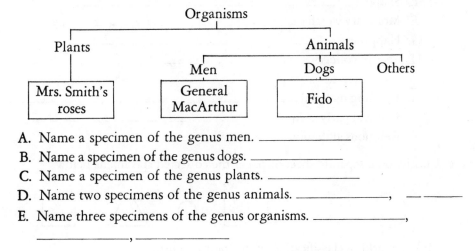

A. Name a specimen of the genus men. _____
B. Name a specimen of the genus dogs. _____
C. Name a specimen of the genus plants. _____
D. Name two specimens of the genus animals. _____, _____
E. Name three specimens of the genus organisms. _____,
   _____, _____

3. Put a circle around the letter of each of the following names which, as com-
   monly used, stands for a specimen.

A. Albert Einstein	G. Africa	M. Actor
B. Nation	H. Star	N. Ford convertible
C. Lawn	I. North America	O. The gun used to
D. Mississippi River	J. Bottle of Coca-Cola	assassinate Lincoln
E. Scientist	K. Chair	P. Venus (the goddess)
F. Venus (the planet)	L. Dollar bill	

4. Here are some sets of vertical sorting factors. Write an appropriate horizontal sorting factor for each set.

    A. Red, yellow, blue _____
    B. Large, medium-sized, small _____
    C. Cold, cool, neutral, warm, hot _____
    D. Sweet, bland, sour, bitter _____
    E. 18th century, 19th century, 20th century _____
    F. Beautiful, plain, ugly _____
    G. Cash, check, money order _____
    H. American, French, Russian, Swedish, Bolivian _____
    I. God, angels, men, animals, plants, matter _____
    J. Agrarian, manufacturing, mercantile _____

5. Here are some horizontal sorting factors. Write two, three, or four appropriate vertical sorting factors, as indicated.

    A. Sex _____, _____
    B. Weight _____, _____
    C. Season _____, _____, _____,

       _____
    D. Mood _____, _____
    E. Shape _____, _____, _____
    F. Monetary worth _____, _____, _____
    G. Happiness _____, _____, _____
    H. Year in college _____, _____, _____,

       _____
    I. Building material _____, _____, _____
    J. Political party _____, _____, _____
    K. Religious affiliation _____, _____, _____

6. Classify on a separate sheet of paper the collected specimens below.

7. Make a working classification of geometric figures.
8. Classify the contents of your pockets or handbag by the stages suggested in section 3-2-1-3.

Conversation Piece

73

9. Now, for extended practice, go to work on the "Conversation Piece" above, the companion list in *C* following, and the following related questions.

   A. If we imagine the "Conversation Piece" without numbers, we could call it a congeries of things. Why?

   B. If we include the numbers in our consideration, we could call it a series (except for the two items that have tumbled in unannounced). Why?

   C. Identify the specimens by placing the appropriate number in the blank beside the specimen name.

1. _____ airplane	15. _____ pick
2. _____ ball-peen hammer	16. _____ pickup truck
3. _____ brace	17. _____ racer
4. _____ coupe	18. _____ rake
5. _____ crescent wrench	19. _____ saw
6. _____ cutlass	20. _____ screwdriver
7. _____ drawknife	21. _____ sickle
8. _____ hatchet	22. _____ sledgehammer
9. _____ jack (Jill)*	23. _____ spade
10. _____ machine gun	24. _____ sports car
11. _____ monkey wrench	25. _____ Stillson wrench
12. _____ Omega**	26. _____ stove bolt
13. _____ panel truck	27. _____ trowel
14. _____ plane	28. _____ try square

   * Jack was disqualified (why?) and Jill was ruled an able-bodied manjack.
   ** Can you think of a reason Omega should be placed at the end of this list?

   D. If classification is "sorting for a purpose," by any stretch of the imagination could the list in *C* be called a classification?

   Yes _____ No _____

   E. If not, why not?

   F. If yes, what might be the purpose?

   G. Name the series in *B* with a more specific term than *things* and give your reason for selecting one of the following terms: *means, devices, instruments, tools.*

   H. If you add a roasted peanut and a live goldfish to the collection, which names, if any, would be eliminated as not suitable?

   I. Name the main sorting factors (vertical) if the horizontal factor at that level is function, and *function* means the role played by a part in achieving the purpose of a whole operation.

   J. Can the objects in the picture be used to illustrate our basic classification of signs? If so, which object would be the best choice for the simple sign category?

   K. Assuming that most of the objects are representations, what would be the best top-level sorting factor if you wish to define the objects they represent?

L. Make a five-level classification that includes all the objects.

M. How many pigeonholes should it have? Why?

N. If the queen can be a chessman, may not Jill be a manjack? After all, isn't everyone a manjack?

3*3

STRUCTURE ANALYSIS

3*3*1

TEXT

3*3*1*1

DEFINITIONS

The analysis of structures will be aided by the use of these four terms: *part, whole, joint,* and *anatomizing factor.*

PARTS AND WHOLES

A whole is a structure; a part is a unit of a structure. A man is a whole composed of parts such as arms and legs. The earth is a whole composed of parts such as sea, atmosphere, crust, and core. The structure of a football game may be thought of as a whole composed of parts such as grandstands, spectators, gridiron, goalposts, and players. Everything which exists may be thought of as a part of the universe as a whole. The words *part* and *whole* signify the relationship of spatial inclusion. Things which are normally considered parts may be thought of, in certain situations, as wholes. A hand, for example, may be called a whole rather than a part if we are concerned with *its* parts. In structure analysis the largest including thing with which we are concerned is called a whole. Its included units are called parts. Thus the United States is a whole country but is also a part of North America; California is a whole state but is also a part of the United States; and the earth is a whole planet but is also a part of the solar system.

The word *part* may signify a subunit as well as a main unit. An arm is a main unit of the human body; a finger is a subunit. Both are called parts. A finger is a part of an arm as well as a part of the body. We may say that a finger is a main part of an arm and a subpart of the body. A fingernail is a main part of a finger, a subpart of an arm, and a sub-subpart of the body. The body is a whole. Arms, fingers, and fingernails are parts, at various levels of inclusion. Structure analysis is the operation of dividing wholes into their constituent units.

JOINTS

A joint is a connection between two or more parts. The border between the United States and Canada is a joint. A shore line is a joint between land and water. The space between two bricks in a brick wall is a joint. The screw surface connecting the stem of a light bulb to its socket is a joint. A joint is any point, line, surface, or space between adjoining parts.

Joints may be actual or projected. A shore line is an actual joint. The border between the United States and Canada is a projected joint, unless it is a bank or shore line. In analyzing structures it is often convenient to project joints — to "draw lines" so that judgments of spatial relationship may be made.

ANATOMIZING FACTORS

An anatomizing factor is the name of a joint or class of joints. Anatomizing factors indicate the places in which structures are divided into parts. The term *state line* is an anatomizing factor when it indicates the division between two states. The word *corner* is an anatomizing factor when it indicates the vertical line made by two adjoining walls. Anatomizing factors come into being when names are given to joints.

Anatomizing factors are often words such as *line, edge, point, end, start, division, joint, connection, surface, plane, crack, space, curve, limit, middle, side,* and *boundary.*

Structures may be analyzed with the aid of anatomizing factors which indicate joints of various sorts. The human body may be analyzed according to the joints between the major bones, according to the connections among the various organs, or according to the connections among the various tissues. A tree may be analyzed according to the connections between the trunk and the branches or according to the connection between the bark and the wood. Any given structure may be analyzed in different ways for different purposes, and sometimes the joints are arbitrary imaginary lines, such as the little boy's "menagerie lion running around the middle of the earth," meaning the equator.

3*3*1*2

SORTS OF STRUCTURE ANALYSES

There are two sorts of structure analyses: analyses of existing structures and analyses of planned structures. A diagram of the human body and a map of a city are analyses of existing structures. An architect's drawings and an inventor's model are analyses of planned structures. Such analyses are often called plans. There are plans for buildings, plans for highways, plans for furniture, plans for automobiles, plans for aircraft, and so forth. The words *blueprint* and *plan* are often synonyms.

Although plans, as exemplified above, are structure analyses, they may involve considerations of classification and operation analysis. A house plan, for example, must take into account sorts of materials and stages of construction as well as purely spatial considerations. In practical situations analysis is often complex, consisting of all three sorts. Certain phases, however, consist primarily of a single sort. Plans, although they involve considerations of classification and operation analysis, are in the present sense structure analyses.

3*31*3

METHOD OF STRUCTURE ANALYSIS

The following stages are suggested for the process of structure analysis:

    I. NAME THE STRUCTURE

    II. NAME THE PURPOSE AND RELEVANT ANATOMIZING FACTORS

    III. DETERMINE AND NAME THE MAIN PARTS

    IV. DETERMINE AND NAME THE MAIN PARTS OF PARTS AS FAR AS NECESSARY TO SERVE THE PURPOSE

It is often fruitful, after determining the purpose of structure analysis, to make a list of possible anatomizing factors before deciding upon a method of taking a structure apart. The question, What are the joints of this? may precede the question, What are the parts of this? Naming the joints of a structure may help to decide what the main parts and sub-parts should be. One might be tempted to say that a chair consists of three main parts: a back, a seat, and legs. But what if the back of the chair and the rear legs are made from a single piece of wood and have no actual joint between them? The main parts might then be the seat, the front legs, and the back with the rear legs. Listing possible anatomizing factors (naming main joints and subjoints) often eliminates the possibility of analyzing a structure according to joints which do not exist. It is important to realize, however, that projected joints sometimes yield useful anatomizing factors. When such factors seem relevant, they should be listed as possibilities. If the purpose of analyzing a chair is to paint it rather than to take it apart or put it together, projected joints might yield useful anatomizing factors. After analysis one might decide to paint the legs of the chair first, then the seat, and then the back, regardless of the fact that the chair might have been constructed of different main parts. A full list of possible anatomizing factors makes possible a choice among them which enables structure analysis to proceed with efficiency and understanding.

The actual process of dividing a structure, existing or planned, into parts may be divided into stages. The first stage involves the division of the structure into main parts. The second stage involves the division of the main parts into subparts. The third and succeeding stages involve continued acts of division.

Take the skeletal position of your hand, for example:

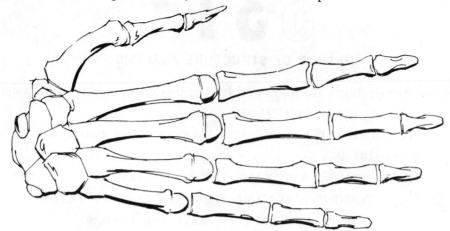

I. Division of structure into main parts. After deciding where your fore-arm stops and your hand begins, you answer the question, What are the *main* parts of the hand? Suppose your answer is wrist, palm, and fingers. But *fingers* is plural, a genus term with five species. Aren't you classifying? You say, "No, I can think of them as one part."

Wrist   Palm   Fingers

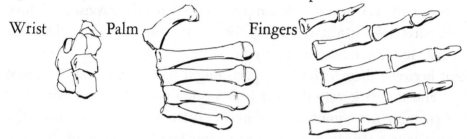

II. Division of main parts into subparts. What are the main parts of the fingers? Your answer is the four fingers and the thumb. (You have changed the sense of *fingers*.)

Fingers   Thumb

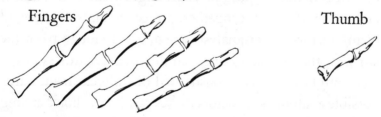

III. Division of subparts into sub-subparts. And what are the main parts of the fingers (new sense)? Answer: forefinger, big finger, ring finger, and little finger.

forefinger   big finger   ring finger   little finger

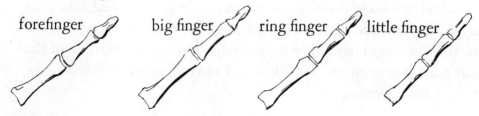

But before we proceed with our hand, this is a handy place for an excursus on the terminology of science. (*Excursus* is merely a Latin word for "related side trip.") You will notice that we have been using English words to name the skeletal parts rather than the terms *metacarpus, phalanges,* and so forth, which you may have learned in school. In fact, there are no special terms in English for the eight bones of the wrist and the fourteen of the fingers. Because science is an international enterprise, scientists have come to agree on the use of Greek and Latin names for their concepts, and we call these naming systems nomenclatures, which means "called names" in Latin. But we have used English names because our major objective is to achieve a clear idea of the three types of analysis which are basic components of every science and because we believe the understanding we seek will come best in the language you think in. Therefore, for the wrist we have translated the various classical terms, but since anatomists simply use *phalanx* ("finger bone") for all fourteen, we made up our own nomenclature for the "palm" and the "grip." We translated the handy terms *proximal* and *distal* as "closer to" and "away from" (the midline of the body) and named the palm bones after the fingers they serve. Here, then, is a complete structure analysis of the bony structure of the hand:

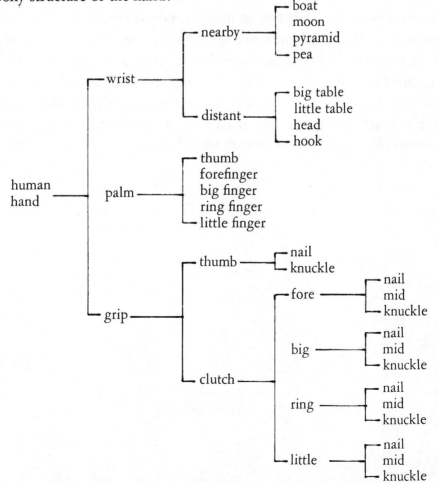

human hand
- wrist
  - nearby
    - boat
    - moon
    - pyramid
    - pea
  - distant
    - big table
    - little table
    - head
    - hook
- palm
  - thumb
  - forefinger
  - big finger
  - ring finger
  - little finger
- grip
  - thumb
    - nail
    - knuckle
  - clutch
    - fore
      - nail
      - mid
      - knuckle
    - big
      - nail
      - mid
      - knuckle
    - ring
      - nail
      - mid
      - knuckle
    - little
      - nail
      - mid
      - knuckle

And here is an "exploded" drawing of the structure as analyzed:

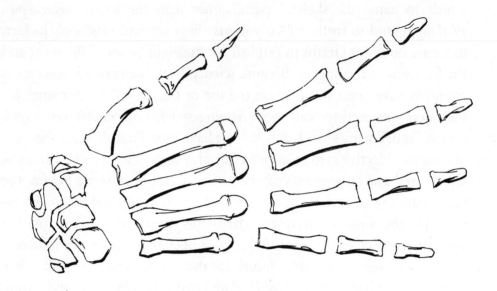

In conclusion, we must emphasize the fundamental difference and the fundamental similarity between *classification* and *structure analysis*. Just as there are no joints in the one, so there are no pigeons in the other. The name of a classification is the name of all the pigeonholes, full or empty, and the pigeons that belong in them. The name of a structure analysis is the name of the entire structure. But language plays a similarly vital part in both the development of our knowledge and our understanding of the world in which we operate. We shall have more to say about the use of old names for things that are new to us in Section 4.

3*3*2

TEXT-RELATED EXERCISES

1. Answer the following questions by referring to the structure anlaysis of the hand on page 81.

    A. What are two main parts of the hand?

    ——————————   ——————————

    B. What are two main parts of the grip?

    ——————————   ——————————

    C. What are two subparts of the wrist?

    ——————————   ——————————

    D. The ring finger is a part of what three things?

    ——————————   ——————————   ——————————

    E. Are the joints actual or projected?

    ——————————

    F. What general name would you give the joints?

    ——————————

2. Each of the phrases below indicates a sort of joint. Place the number of each phrase in the appropriate pigeonhole of the diagram.

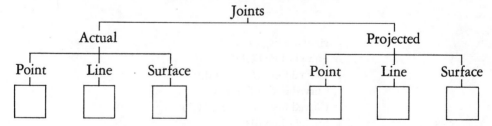

Joints

    Actual   Projected

Point   Line   Surface   Point   Line   Surface

    A. City limits
    B. The area of contact between the kneecap and the bones of the leg
    C. The imaginary plane dividing the human body into a right half and a left half
    D. The part of a man's hair
    E. The apex of a triangle
    F. The apogee of an earth satellite

3. The abstract drawing below is followed by two structure analyses. At the top of each level is a parenthesis. In each parenthesis write the letter of the appropriate anatomizing factor.

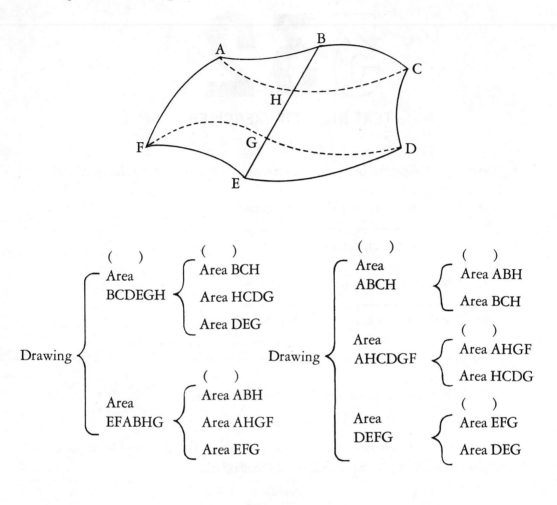

Anatomizing factors

A. Straight line EGHB
B. Curved lines HC and GD
C. Curved lines AH and FG
D. Curved lines AHC and FGD
E. Straight line BH
F. Straight line HG
G. Straight line GE

4. Suppose that you are flying over a group of islands and that one of them resembles the drawing that follows. Make a structure analysis of the island so that you'll be able to recognize it again (it's the only one with friendly natives). Be sure to include anatomizing factors.

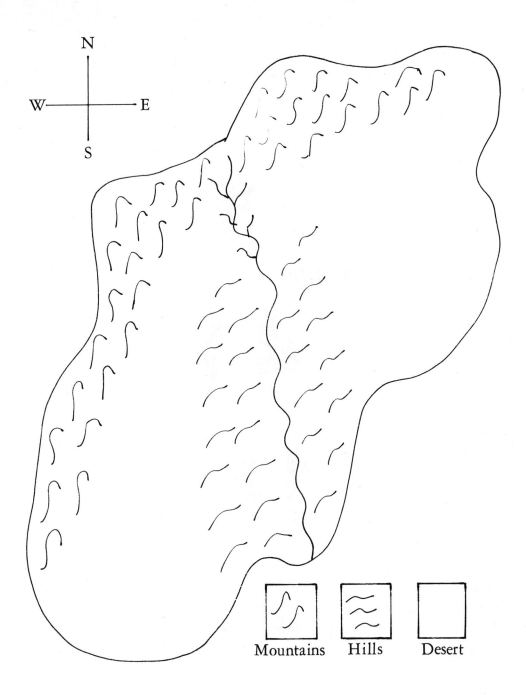

Mountains Hills Desert

5. Name three existing structures and three structures that a person might plan.

Existing	Planned
A. _____	a. _____
B. _____	b. _____
C. _____	c. _____

6. Analyze the structure of a pencil or pen by the method suggested in Section 3-3-1-3.

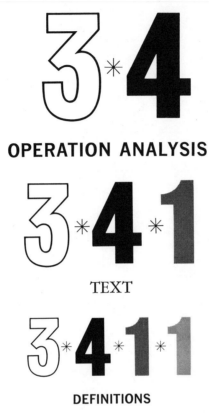

OPERATION ANALYSIS

TEXT

DEFINITIONS

The analysis of operations will be aided by the use of these terms: *stage, operation, juncture, ordering factor,* and *purpose.* (*Phase* and *function,* which are terms used in a special sort of operation analysis, will be discussed in the phase analysis portion of this section.)

STAGES AND OPERATIONS

An *operation* is a structure changing in time and space for a purpose. A *stage* is a temporal unit of an operation. A football game, for example, is an operation consisting of stages such as the first quarter and the second quarter. The changing structure consists of parts such as the field, the players, the goalposts, and the spectators. The interaction of the parts for a certain period of time is the operation. The interaction of the parts for a unit of the total time is a stage of the operation. Telephoning, as another example, is an operation consisting of stages such as dialing and speaking. The changing structure consists of parts such as the telephone, the caller, and the telephone lines. The operation is made up of changing parts such as the moving dial, the moving lips of the caller, and the moving current on the telephone lines. The stages of the operation are main parts of the total period of change. During the dialing stage the dial moves but the lips of the caller remain still, as far as speech is concerned. During the speaking stage the lips of the caller move but the dial does not. Stages are usually characterized by certain sorts of change. The beginning of a new sort of change marks the beginning of a new stage.

The words *stage* and *operation* signify the relationship of temporal inclusion. Things which are considered operations may be thought of, in certain situations, as stages and *vice versa.* The first half of a football game may be called an operation rather than a stage if we are not concerned with the second half. On the other hand a football game may be called a stage rather than an operation if we are concerned with related events, such as a parade and dance, which may come before and after the game. In operation analysis the longest inclusive event with which we are concerned is called an operation. Its included temporal units are called stages.

The word *stage* may signify a subunit as well as a main unit of an operation. The first half of a football game is a main unit; the first quarter is a subunit. Both are called stages. The first quarter is a stage of the first half as well as a stage of the football game. We may say that the first quarter is a main stage of the first half and a substage of the football game. The opening kickoff is a main stage of the first quarter, a substage of the first half, and a sub-substage of the football game. A football game is an operation; the first half, the first quarter, and the kickoff are stages, at various levels of inclusion. Operation analysis is the operation of dividing operations into their constituent temporal units.

JUNCTURES

Junctures are points of division between stages, much as joints are places of division between parts. A juncture is the point in time when one stage ends and another begins. When the minute hand of a clock points to 12, one hour-long stage in the operation of the clock has ended and another is about to begin. The position of the minute hand and of the other parts constitutes a juncture between the two stages. A juncture is any position of the changing structure regarded as the beginning or end of a stage. Some junctures are considered more important than others. The position of the parts of a clock at 5:27 is a juncture but the position at 5:00 may be considered a more important one. Thus 5:00 marks the beginning of a main stage (an hour) and 5:27 marks the beginning of a substage (a minute). The juncture which exists when the bullet shot from a hunter's rifle is one foot away from a deer may be considered less important than the juncture which exists when the bullet is first in contact with the deer's body. Thus we are likely to say that the wounding or killing stage of hunting begins with the second juncture rather than with the first. Any meaningful arrangement of the parts of a changing structure is a juncture from some point of view. Significant arrangements mark the beginnings and ends of main stages of change while arrangements of secondary importance mark the beginnings and ends of substages of change.

ORDERING FACTORS

An ordering factor is a term which indicates a juncture or a number of junctures. Ordering factors indicate the points in time by which operations are divided into stages. The word *hour* is an ordering factor when it indicates the junctures by which the operation of a clock is divided into stages. *Hour* stands for twelve different junctures, twelve different positions in the operation of a clock. The operation of a clock is analyzed *according to* its hours. The word *minute* is an ordering factor when it indicates the junctures by which an hour is divided into substages. *Minute* stands for sixty different junctures, sixty different positions of the minute hand and other parts of the clock. An hour is analyzed *according to* its minutes. The word *impact* is an ordering factor when it indicates the juncture by which the flight of a missile and its consequent destruction are divided into stages. *Impact* stands for a single juncture, a single position in the operation of a missile. The operation of a missile is analyzed *according to* its impact. The word *touchdown* is an ordering factor when it indicates the position of a football, together with the positions of the other parts of a football game, when it has been grounded for a score. *Touchdown* stands for a juncture between past and coming stages in a football game. Events in a football game are analyzed *according to* touchdowns. Ordering factors come into being when names are given to junctures or sorts of junctures.

PURPOSES

We have defined an operation as having a *purpose.* The purpose of an operation is the reason for its existence. One operation may have several purposes, of course. Reading a newspaper may be done for entertainment, for information, as part of a research project, and so on. The purpose of an operation often differs from the purpose of an analysis of that operation. The purpose of a clock is to keep time. The purpose of an operation analysis of that clock may be to determine *how* it keeps time. The purpose of a football game may be entertainment; the purpose of an operation analysis of it may be to determine the strengths and weaknesses of various plays or players. The purpose of our analysis determines our choice of ordering factors, just as it did our choice of sorting and anatomizing factors. Any given operation may be analyzed in different ways for different purposes.

3*4*1*2

SORTS OF OPERATION ANALYSES

There are two sorts of operation analyses: analyses of past operations and analyses of planned operations. A history of the Civil War and a record of an earthquake are analyses of past operations. An author's outline and a building contractor's work schedule are analyses of planned operations. Such analyses are often called *plans*. A plan indicates stages of a planned operation. A floor plan or a plan of the structure of a chair is not a plan in this operational sense. Plans are analyses which indicate *how* to build a house or *how* to build a chair. Plans indicate *when* to do *what*. Analyses of past operations indicate what has been done or what has happened. In analyzing a past operation one discovers junctures and then determines stages and substages. In making a plan one determines the junctures, as well as the stages and the substages.

3*4*1*3

METHOD OF OPERATION ANALYSIS

The process of operation analysis may be divided into the following stages:

      I. NAME THE OPERATION
     II. DETERMINE THE PURPOSE AND RELEVANT ORDERING
        FACTORS
    III. DIVIDE THE OPERATION INTO STAGES
        A. MAIN STAGES
        B. SUBSTAGES
          OTHERS

It is often fruitful, after determining the purpose of analysis, to make a list of possible ordering factors before deciding upon a method of dividing an operation into stages. The question, "What are the junctures of this?" may precede the question, "What are the stages of this?" Naming the principle junctures of an operation may help an individual decide what the main stages and substages should be. Important junctures exist when two or more parts or aspects of parts assume important positions with respect to each other. A sunset is an important juncture because a part, the sun, and an aspect of a part, the perceived edge of the earth, come together. The word *sunset* is an ordering factor if it indicates the division between night and day. The arrival of the sun at its zenith is an important juncture because a part, the sun, and an aspect of a part, a point on earth, assume the position of being directly above and below each other. The word *zenith* is an ordering factor if it indicates a division between morning and afternoon. The arrival of a ship at the Panama Canal is an important juncture because two parts, a ship and the canal, come together. The phrase *arrival at the Panama Canal* is an ordering factor if it indicates a division between an Atlantic and a Pacific stage of a voyage. Important junctures are points of contact, positions of nearness or farness, or moments of significant interrelationship among parts or aspects of parts. Ordering factors name junctures which divide operations into stages.

Let us imagine that we are taking a space flight through the solar system. Leaving earth our first stop is the moon. From the moon we fly past Venus and land on Mercury. From Mercury we fly past Venus, past earth and land on Mars. We then return to earth. Before deciding upon a method of dividing this operation into stages, let us name the principal junctures. The operation has three junctures of contact and three junctures of proximity. The space ship comes in contact with the moon, Mercury, and Mars; it comes near Venus twice and near the earth once. This information will enable us to decide which junctures should divide main stages and which should divide substages. Here are three possible analyses:

1	**2**	**3**

I. Earth to moon
II. Moon to Mercury
   A. Moon to vicinity of Venus
   B. Vicinity of Venus to Mercury
III. Mercury to Mars
   A. Mercury to vicinity of Venus
   B. Vicinity of Venus to vicinity of earth
   C. Vicinity of earth to Mars
IV. Mars to earth

I. Earth to Mercury
   A. Earth to vicinity of Venus
     a. Earth to moon
     b. Moon to vicinity of Venus
   B. Vicinity of Venus to Mercury
II. Mercury to Mars
   A. Mercury to vicinity of Venus
   B. Vicinity of Venus to vicinity of earth
   C. Vicinity of earth to Mars
III. Mars to earth

I. Earth to vicinity of Venus
   A. Earth to moon
   B. Moon to vicinity of Venus
II. Vicinity of Venus to vicinity of Venus
   A. Vicinity of Venus to Mercury
   B. Mercury to vicinity of Venus
III. Vicinity of Venus to vicinity of earth
IV. Vicinity of earth to earth
   A. Vicinity of earth to Mars
   B. Mars to earth

In the first analysis the ordering factor for the first vertical level (or column) is *points of contact.* The ordering factor for the level under II is *vicinity of Venus.* The ordering factor for the level under III is *vicinities of Venus and earth.* In the second analysis the ordering factor for the first level is *points of contact with planets.* The ordering factor for the level under I is *vicinity of Venus.* The ordering factor for the level under I-A is *contact with the moon.* The ordering factor for the level under II is *vicinities of Venus and earth.* In the third analysis the ordering factor for the first level is *points of vicinity.* The ordering factor for the level under I is *contact with the moon.* The ordering factor for the level under II is *contact with Mercury.* The ordering factor for the level under IV is *contact with Mars.*

If we are interested primarily in points of contact and secondarily in positions of proximity, we will use the first analysis. If we are interested primarily in points of contact with planets, secondarily with positions of proximity with planets, and thirdly with the point of contact with the moon, we will use the second analysis. If we are interested primarily in positions of proximity and secondarily in points of contact, we will use the third analysis. The first analysis might be appropriate if the purpose of the journey is to deliver supplies to the moon, Mercury, and Mars. The second, if the purpose is to obtain geological samples from Mercury and Mars, in which case getting to the moon might be considered a mere substage of getting to Mercury. The third would be best if the purpose is to get high altitude photographs of Venus and the earth, in which case junctures with other bodies may be considered of minor importance.

Any operation may be analyzed in different ways for different purposes. By listing principal junctures and considering possible ordering factors we enable ourselves to choose methods of analysis which are appropriate to our particular purposes.

The actual process of dividing an operation, past or planned, into stages may itself be divided into stages. The first stage involves the division of the operation into main stages. The second stage involves the division of the main stages into substages. The third and succeeding stages involve continued acts of division. The operation of hunting has been analyzed in stages below.

> I. Division of operation into main stages
>   (Stalking, Shooting, Retrieving)
> II. Division of main stages into substages
>   A. Division of main stage 1 into substages
>   (Stalking divided into Tracking, Sighting, and Approaching)
>   B. Division of main stage 2 into substages
>   (Shooting divided into Aiming, Firing, and
>   Wounding or Killing)
> III. Division of substages into sub-substages
>   (Firing divided into Squeezing of trigger, Explosion of charge,
>   and Recoil and flight of bullet)

Here is a diagram summarizing the result of this analytic process.

> Hunting
>   I. Stalking
>   A. Tracking
>   B. Sighting
>   C. Approaching
>   II. Shooting
>   A. Aiming
>   B. Firing
>   1. Squeezing of trigger
>   2. Explosion of charge
>   3. Recoil and flight of bullet
>   C. Wounding or Killing of game
>   III. Retrieving

Other methods of representing analyzed operations are also possible. With appropriate notations a series of pictures representing junctures may indicate an analyzed operation. A motion picture may also serve this purpose. Or an analyzed operation may be represented in the spatial rather than in the temporal dimension. Thus the orbit of an earth satellite may be represented by an ellipse drawn on a sheet of paper or the operation of a beating heart may be represented by the jagged line of an electrocardiogram. An analyzed operation may be represented by any method which indicates stages or stages and phases.

Because the mind operates best with small numbers of items, an operation should, in most cases, be divided into no more than six or seven main stages, and a stage of an operation should be divided into no more than six or seven constituent stages. The operation of hunting, analyzed above, might have been divided at the start into the following stages:

Tracking
Sighting
Approaching
Aiming
Squeezing of trigger
Explosion of charge
Recoil and flight of bullet
Wounding or Killing of game
Retrieving

But the operation is easier to comprehend and to remember by the use, at various levels of inclusion, of words such as *stalking, shooting,* and *firing.* The division of an hour into sixty minutes seems to violate the rule that more than six or seven stages at any one level of an operation analysis is too many. But custom has categorized the minutes of an hour into twelve divisions of five, four divisions of fifteen, and two divisions of thirty. Thus in telling time an hour is normally analyzed so that a given level consists of no more than five stages. By the process of division and subdivision operations of vast complexity may be analyzed with comparative ease.

3*4*1*4

PHASE ANALYSIS

In analyzing complex operations it is often useful to focus on the parts of the structure to see how their particular functions interact and contribute to the purpose of the entire operation. Thus, in addition to dividing an operation into temporal units, we may also divide it into part units. A *phase* of an operation is the functioning of one part during an operation. A *phase analysis* is the operation of dividing phases into the same temporal units as the operation analysis of the whole structure, so that the relationships among the parts and the whole may be determined. Considering the functioning of the center, the halfback, the quarterback, and other players during a football game would enable a coach to pinpoint the reasons for the success or failure of the plays. Considering the functioning of the home team, the visiting team, the spectators, and so forth would help campus security officers plan traffic and crowd control. Just as the purpose of the operation analysis determines the limits and the stages of an operation, so the purpose of the phase analysis determines which parts of the structure are relevant to any particular analysis.

THE RELATIONSHIP OF OPERATIONS AND PHASES

Operations have purposes; phases, or moving parts of operations, have functions. The purpose of an operation is the reason for its existence; the function of a phase is its contribution to the reason or "end" of the operation. The purpose of a baseball game may be entertainment, exercise, or a combination of such values. The function of the phase of the bat, or of the bats if there are many, is to hit the ball. But if the purpose of the operation is exercise, the function of the moving bat, to this end, may also be to serve as a weight which exercises the arms. We may say that the purpose of the operation of an internal combustion engine is to translate the energy of gasoline into motion of the flywheel. The function of the phase of the carburetor is to produce an explosive mixture of gasoline and air. This mixing function of the carburetor phase is an essential contribution to the achievement of the purpose of the operation of the engine. Each "functional" part of the structure of an operation plays an essential or beneficial role in achieving the operation's purpose. The chrome trim on an automobile is a functionless part when the purpose of the operating car is transportation. But the trim may be vitally functional in the larger operation of a man's life, in which considerations of beauty and status may be relevant. Functions and purposes answer such questions as "What does it do?" and "What is it for?"

The purpose of an operation may become the function of a phase if attention is shifted to a more comprehensive operation. The purpose of the operation of an internal combustion engine, to change chemical energy into kinetic energy (the energy of motion), becomes a function when we think of the part the engine plays in the operation of an automobile. During World War II the purpose of the munitions industry, the manufacture of armaments, was also a function in the larger operation of the war effort. The purposes of our various activities are functions which contribute to the purposes of our lives. Purposes become functions when operations become phases, or when changing structures become changing parts. Purposes are the reasons for change in occurrences which are considered operations; functions are the contributions of phases to the purposes of operations.

METHOD OF PHASE ANALYSIS

The analysis of an operation in which phases are relevant presents a special problem. Each phase in the operation may be treated as an operation in itself. Thus it may be analyzed in the same way that an operation is analyzed. It is often useful, however, to indicate the relationships among phases. It may be desirable to know what stages in two or more phases occur at the same time and how they contribute to an integrated stage of the total operation. In the operation of walking, for example, the left foot supports the body while the right foot strides forward. The support stage of the phase of the left foot, together with the stride stage of the phase of the right, combine to form a stage in the operation of walking. The auricles of the heart fill with blood while the ventricles pump blood into the arteries. These stages of the auricle and ventricle phases combine to make the systole stage of the total operation of the heart. An usherette in a theatre shows latecomers to their seats while the projectionist runs the film. These stages of the usherette and projectionist phases, together with other stages of other phases, may contribute to the "main feature" stage of the total operation of a theatre for an evening.

The indication of a complex operation and its phases and their inter-relations may proceed as follows. The total operation may be divided into stages and substages. Each phase may be divided into stages and substages. Then the separate analyses may be placed side by side so as to indicate the temporal relationships among their various stages. The names of stages in the various phases will be parallel to each other. The names of stages of the operation will be parallel to the names of the stages of the phases and will act in a comprehensive manner, as "generalizations" for the names of the stages of the phases.

A phase analysis of the operation of walking follows.

PHASE ANALYSIS OF THE OPERATION OF WALKING

Walking	Phase of left foot	Phase of right foot
I. First cycle of walking	I. First cycle of left foot	I. First cycle of right foot
A. Right stride stage (including what the left foot does)	A. Support	A. Stride
B. Left stride stage (including what the right foot does)	B. Stride	B. Support
II. Second cycle of walking	II. Second cycle of left foot	II. Second cycle of right foot
A. Right stride stage	A. Support	A. Stride
B. Left stride stage	B. Stride	B. Support
Other cycles	Other cycles	Other cycles

TEXT-RELATED EXERCISES

1. Answer the following questions by referring to the diagram below.

> Hunting
>> I. Stalking
>> II. Shooting
>>> A. Aiming
>>> B. Firing
>> III. Retrieving

A. What are two stages of shooting? _____, _____

B. What are three main stages of hunting? _____,

_____, _____

C. What are two substages of hunting? _____, _____

D. Firing is a stage of what two things? _____, _____

2. Name three stages and three phases of the operations indicated below. Remember that a phase is the motion of a *part* of a structure.

A. Baseball game

Stages _____, _____, _____

Phases _____, _____, _____

B. Construction of a house

Stages _____, _____, _____

Phases _____, _____, _____

C. Biological evolution

Stages _____, _____, _____

Phases _____, _____, _____

D. History of America

Stages _____, _____, _____

Phases _____, _____, _____

3. Describe two primary and two secondary junctures of each operation indicated below. Remember that junctures mark the endings and beginnings of stages.

A. The swinging of a pendulum

Primary _____, _____

Secondary _____, _____

B. A bath

Primary _____, _____

Secondary _____, _____

C. World War II

Primary _____, _____

Secondary _____, _____

4. Name three possible ordering factors for each operation indicated below.

   A. Getting dressed _____, _____, _____

   B. Vacation _____, _____, _____

   C. Writing and mailing
   a letter _____, _____, _____

5. On a separate sheet of paper name three phases and their functions and three operations and their purposes. Then name three larger operations in which the three operations may be phases and their purposes may be functions.

6. Name three past operations and three operations which a person might plan.

7. Analyze the operation of buying groceries by the stages suggested in section 3-4-1-3.

8. List three operations which might be analyzed by phase analysis. Then analyze one of them.

EXERCISES IN THE APPLICATION OF ANALYSIS

FILL-IN DIAGRAMS

In working the following exercises, add horizontal sorting factors to the classi-fications, anatomizing factors to the structure analyses, and ordering factors to the operation analyses. Assign a possible purpose to each analysis.

1 Place the terms below on the appropriate lines of the diagram.

    _____

      I. _____

        A. _____

        B. _____

     II. _____

   III. _____

        A. _____

        B. _____

1. Cleaning brushes
2. Applying paint to chair
3. Preparation
4. Buying paint
5. Painting a chair
6. Putting away leftover paint, brushes, and other implements
7. Cleaning up
8. Mixing paint

2 Place the sorting factors below on the appropriate lines of the diagram and place the letters of the specimens in the appropriate pigeonholes.

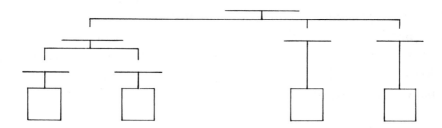

SORTING FACTORS:
1. Pantheistic
2. Monotheistic
3. Materialistic
4. Theistic
5. Beliefs concerning the existence of divinity in the universe
6. Polytheistic

SPECIMENS:
a. God is everywhere: in the rocks, in the trees, and in the souls of men.
b. God is the creator of the world.
c. There are many gods who rule the world but are not a part of it.
d. There are no supernatural forces in the universe.

3 Place the terms below on the appropriate lines of the diagram.

1. Field of stars
2. Red stripes
3. Stars
4. American flag
5. Stripes
6. Blue background
7. White stripes

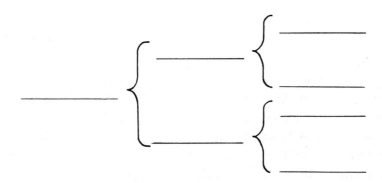

4 Place the terms below on the appropriate lines of the diagram.

1. Contact
2. Bat recoils from contact with ball.
3. Bat hits ball.
4. Phase of bat
5. Recoil of bat and flight of ball
6. Bat swings across plate.

7. Phase of ball
8. Ball hits bat.
9. Hitting of baseball
10. Ball moves through air to vicinity of batter's box.
11. Pitch and swing

_____	_____	_____
I. _____	I. _____	I. _____
II. _____	II. _____	II. _____
III. _____	III. _____	III. Ball bounces from bat and flies through air.

5 Place the sorting factors below on the appropriate lines of the diagram and place the letters of the specimens in the appropriate pigeonholes.

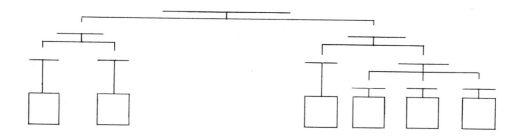

SORTING FACTORS:

1. Eastern
2. Nations
3. European
4. Far Eastern
5. Near Eastern
6. American
7. Western
8. North American
9. West Indian
10. South American

SPECIMENS:

a. United States
b. England
c. Red China
d. Egypt
e. France
f. Mexico
g. Brazil
h. Cuba

6 Place the terms below on the appropriate lines of the diagram.

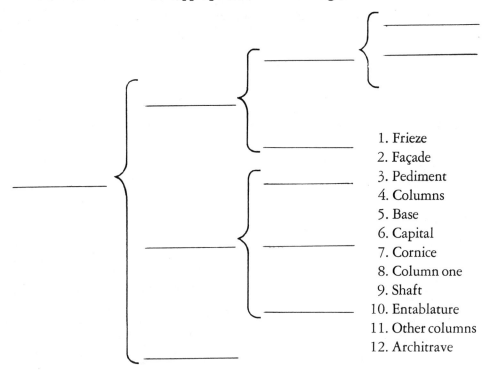

1. Frieze
2. Façade
3. Pediment
4. Columns
5. Base
6. Capital
7. Cornice
8. Column one
9. Shaft
10. Entablature
11. Other columns
12. Architrave

7 Place the terms below on the appropriate lines of the diagram. One of the terms is ambiguous and may be used more than once.

_____

A. _____

B. _____

   1. _____

      a. _____

      b. _____

      c. _____

   2. _____

      a. _____

      b. _____

      c. _____

   3. _____

      a. _____

      b. _____

      c. _____

C. _____

1. Adulthood
2. Old age
3. Youth
4. Late childhood
5. Teen years
6. Life
7. Childhood
8. Attainment of legal maturity
   (common law)
9. Death
10. Middle age
11. Middle childhood
12. Birth
13. Infancy
14. Pre-teen adolescence
15. Young adulthood

8 Place the sorting factors below on the appropriate lines of the diagram and place the letters of the specimens in the appropriate pigeonholes.

SORTING FACTORS:

1. Music
2. German
3. Religious
4. Prose
5. Physics
6. Architecture
7. Scientific
8. Painting
9. Roman
10. Famous works
11. Artistic
12. Secular
13. Mathematics
14. Sculpture
15. Biology
16. Novels
17. Philosophical
18. Plays
19. Greek
20. Writing
21. American
22. Poetry
23. Psychology
24. Essays
25. Chemistry

SPECIMENS:

a. *The Republic,* by Plato
b. *The Divine Comedy,* by Dante
c. *On Friendship,* by Montaigne
d. *The Mona Lisa,* by Leonardo da Vinci
e. *The Marriage of Figaro,* by Mozart
f. *Origin of Species,* by Darwin
g. *New System of Chemistry,* by John Dalton
h. *Some Problems in Philosophy,* by William James
i. *Hamlet,* by Shakespeare
j. *Critique of Practical Reason,* by Kant
k. The Parthenon
l. *The Meaning of Relativity,* by Albert Einstein
m. *Smoke and Steel,* by Sandburg
n. *The Principles of Psychology,* by William James
o. *Discobolus,* by Myron (5th century Greek sculptor)
p. *Meditations,* by Marcus Aurelius
q. *East of Eden,* by Steinbeck
r. *Geometry,* by Descartes

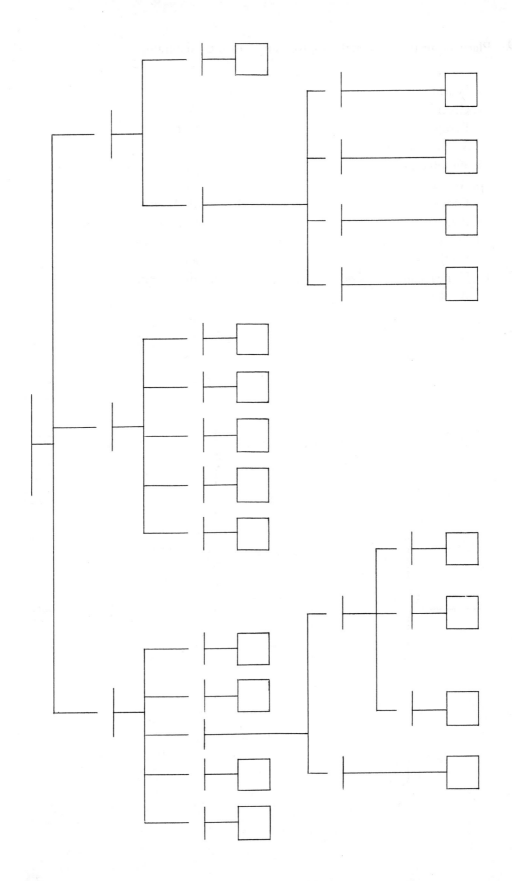

9 Place the terms below on the appropriate lines of the diagram.

1. World
2. Greenland
3. Europe
4. South America
5. West Indies
6. Africa
7. Eurasia
8. Asia
9. Latin America exclusive of South America
10. United States exclusive of Alaska
11. Land
12. Alaska
13. Antarctica
14. Ocean
15. Mexico
16. Australia
17. North America exclusive of Latin American countries
18. Central America
19. Canada
20. North America

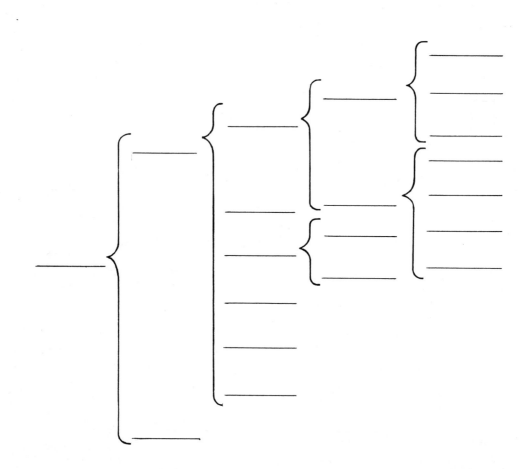

10 Place the terms below on the appropriate lines of the diagram.

_____   1. Mesozoic

1 _____   2. Cambrian

    A _____   3. Pleistocene

    B _____   4. Tertiary

2 _____   5. Pre-Cambrian

    A _____   6. Recent

    B _____   7. Cenozoic

    C _____   8. Geological development of the earth

    D _____   9. Cretaceous

    E _____   10. Silurian

    F _____   11. Eocene (and Paleocene)

3 _____   12. Carboniferous

    A _____   13. Archeozoic

    B _____   14. Miocene

    C _____   15. Pliocene

4 _____   16. Triassic

    A _____   17. Proterozoic

        1 _____   18. Quaternary

        2 _____   19. Jurassic

        3 _____   20. Permian

        4 _____   21. Devonian

    B _____   22. Paleozoic

        1 _____   23. Oligocene

        2 _____   24. Ordovician

11 Place the sorting factors below on the appropriate lines of the diagram and place the letters of the specimens in the appropriate pigeonholes.

SORTING FACTORS:
1. Banishment
2. Involving restriction of action in society
3. Of money
4. Involving physical hurt or destruction
5. Involving social degradation or humiliation
6. Cruel
7. Forms of civil punishment
8. Suspension of rights or privileges
9. Involving economic loss
10. Maiming
11. Of property
12. Humane (involving a minimum of pain)
13. Imprisonment
14. Execution
15. Enslavement or forced labor
16. Torture
17. Captivation

SPECIMENS:
a. Confiscation of belongings
b. Fining
c. Cutting off hands
d. Placing on public display in stocks
e. Deportation
f. Hanging
g. Cutting out tongue
h. Placing in jail
i. Whipping
j. Blinding
k. Crucifixion
l. Hanging by thumbs
m. Indentured slavery
n. Electrocution
o. Burning at stake
p. Suspension of licenses or permits
q. Placing in "chain gangs"
r. Execution in gas chamber
s. Sending to "salt mines"
t. Placing on the rack

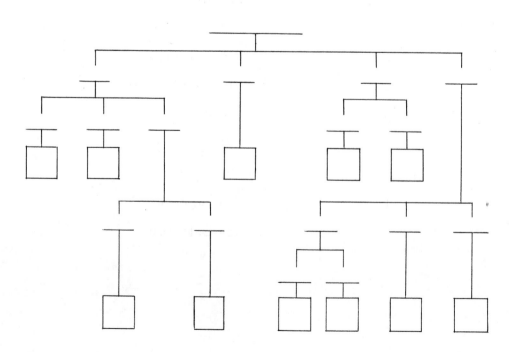

12 Place the terms below on the appropriate lines of the diagram. The word *flower* is ambiguous and may be used more than once.

1. Stem
2. Corolla
3. Sepal #1
4. Carpel #1
5. Sporophylls
6. Petal #5
7. Root
8. Ovule
9. Ovary
10. Sepal #2
11. Rootlets

12. Stamen #1
13. Anther
14. Petal #4
15. Locule
16. Perianth
17. Leaves
18. Petal #3
19. Sepal #5
20. Petal #2
21. Main root
22. Flower

23. Sepal #4
24. Style
25. Receptacle
26. Petal #1
27. Outer wall of ovary
28. Calyx
29. Sepal #3
30. Filament
31. Stigma
32. Stamens
33. Carpels

Etc.

Etc.

13 Place the terms below in the appropriate spaces of the diagram.

1. Chamber dilates and receives blood from pulmonary vein system.
2. Phase of systemic vein system
3. Blood received from left ventricle is conveyed at high pressure to all parts of body except lungs.
4. Phase of right ventricle
5. Systole
6. Blood passes from chamber to right ventricle. Chamber contracts toward end of phase.
7. Blood received from left ventricle is conveyed at low pressure to all parts of body except lungs.
8. Circulation cycle
9. Phase of left auricle
10. Blood is forced into systemic artery system by contraction of ventricle.
11. Chamber dilates and receives blood from right auricle.
12. Chamber dilates and receives blood from systemic vein system.
13. Blood received from right ventricle is conveyed at high pressure to lungs.
14. Diastole
15. Chamber dilates and receives blood from left auricle.
16. Phase of pulmonary artery system
17. Blood from lungs is conveyed to left auricle.
18. Blood from all parts of body except lungs is conveyed to right auricle.
19. Blood is forced into pulmonary artery system by contraction of ventricle.

Phase of right auricle		Phase of left ventricle		Phase of pulmonary vein system	Phase of systemic artery system
a	*a*	*a*	*a*	*a*	*a*
b	*b*	*b* Blood passes from chamber to left ventricle. Chamber contracts toward end of phase.	*b* Blood received from right ventricle is conveyed at low pressure to lungs.	*b* Same as above	*b* Same as above

111

14 Place the sorting factors below on the appropriate lines of the diagram and place the letters of the specimens in the appropriate pigeonholes. The specimens are quotations from the entry under *eye* in *Webster's New World Dictionary.*

SORTING FACTORS:

1. Relevant to perception
2. Rel. to organs of light-sensitivity
3. Rel. to parts of non-living natural things
4. Rel. to the general act or power of seeing
5. Which are light-sensitive
6. Rel. to natural things and their aspects
7. Rel. to immaterial aspects of manufactured objects
8. V. t.
9. Rel. to the iris part of the organ of vision
10. Rel. to non-visual light-sensitive organs
11. Rel. to the power of judgment
12. Senses of *eye*
13. Rel. to manufactured objects and their material aspects
14. Rel. to the entire organ of vision
15. V. i.
16. Rel. to aspects of recreational objects
17. Rel. to parts of vegetables
18. Rel. to non-organ aspects of surface parts of animals
19. Manual
20. Rel. to manufactured things and their aspects
21. Rel. to general perception
22. Rel. to judgment
23. Rel. to a particular visual act
24. Rel. to objects of practical usefulness
25. Rel. to the eyeball part of the organ of vision
26. Concrete
27. Rel. to the state of judgment
28. Which are not light-sensitive
29. N.
30. Rel. to the area of skin surrounding the outer surface of the organ of vision
31. Rel. to the organ of vision
32. Visual
33. Rel. to vision

SPECIMENS:

a. Organ of sight in man and animals
b. The eyeball
c. The iris: as, she has brown *eyes*
d. The area around the eye, including the eyelids: as, he was fighting and got a black *eye*
e. Sight; vision
f. A look; glance; gaze: as, cast your *eye* on this
g. Attention; regard; observation
h. The power of judging, estimating, discriminating, etc. by eyesight: as, a good *eye* for distances
i. *Often in pl.* judgment; opinion; estimation: as, in the *eyes* of the law
j. A bud of a potato
k. The spot on a peacock's tail feather
l. The center of a target; bull's-eye
m. A hole in a tool, as for a handle
n. The threading hole in a needle
o. A loop of metal or thread
p. An organ sensitive to light, as in certain lower forms of life
q. A photoelectric cell
r. In *meteorology,* the calm, low-pressure center (of a hurricane), around which winds of high velocity move
s. To look at; observe; watch carefully; scrutinize
t. To provide with eyes, or holes
u. [Obs.], to appear (to the eyes)

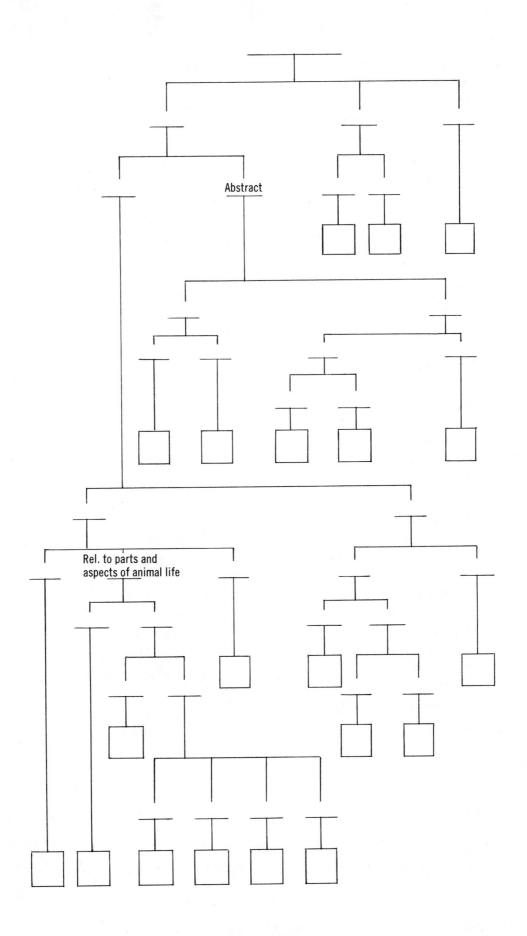

Abstract

Rel. to parts and
aspects of animal life

113

15   Place the terms below on the appropriate lines of the diagram. The term
phalanges may be used twice.

1. Coccyx
2. Hand
3. Chest
4. Foot
5. Axial skeleton or skeleton of
   the head and trunk
6. False ribs
7. Legs
8. Metacarpus
9. Arm shaft
10. Skull
11. Human skeleton
12. Manubrium
13. Leg shaft
14. Fibula
15. Phalanges
16. Carpus
17. Clavicle
18. Forearm
19. Cervical vertebrae
20. True ribs
21. Right upper extremity
22. Little finger
23. Metatarsus
24. Face bones
25. Left upper extremity
26. Fingers
27. Thumb
28. Mesosternum
29. Knee bone or patella

30. Upper arm or humerus
31. Sacrum
32. Arm
33. Lower extremities
34. Tarsus
35. Spine
36. Ribs
37. Appendicular skeleton or
    skeleton of the limbs
38. Index finger
39. Right leg
40. Ulna
41. Floating false ribs
42. Sternum
43. Cranium
44. Lower leg bones
45. Tibia
46. Pelvic girdle
    (exclusive of sacrum)
47. Upper extremities
48. Scapula
49. Thigh bone or femur
50. Thoracic vertebrae
51. Attached false ribs
52. Shoulder
53. Middle finger
54. Xiphoid process
55. Lumbar vertebrae
56. Radius
57. Left leg
58. Ring finger

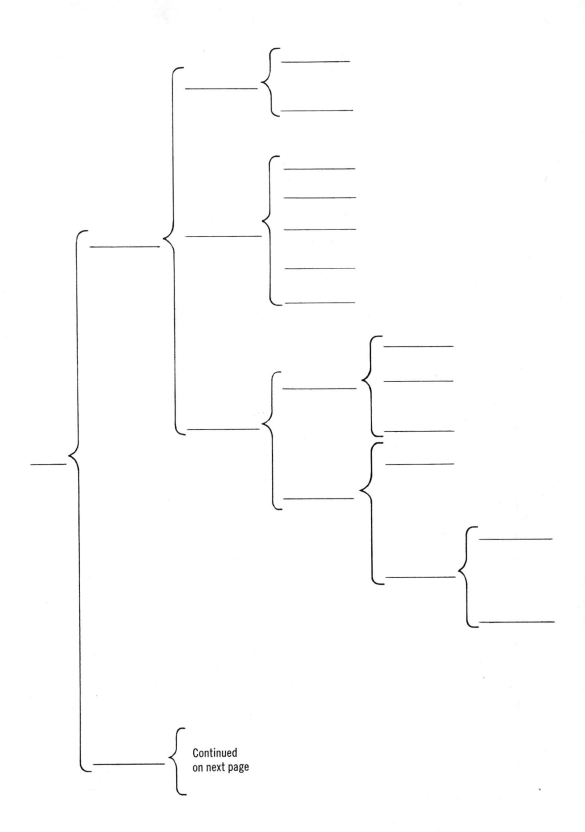

Continued
on next page

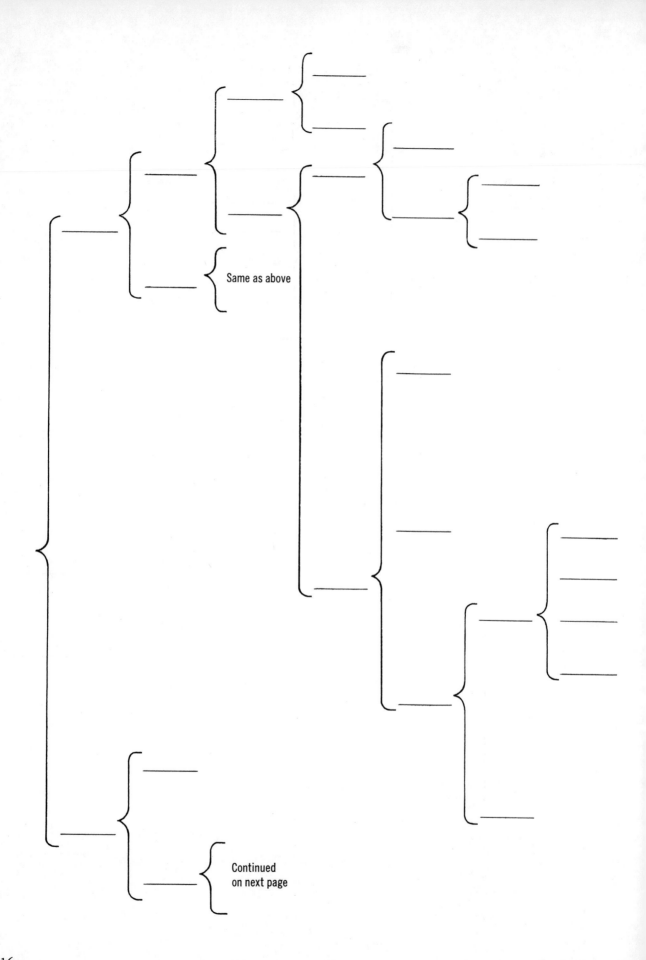

Same as above

Continued
on next page

116

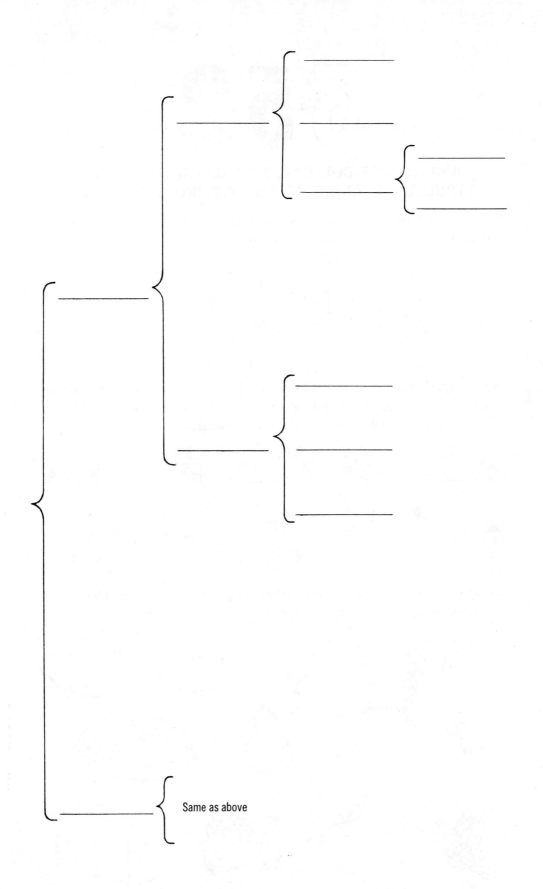

Same as above

3*5*2

ANALYSIS OF COLLECTED SPECIMENS, EXISTING STRUCTURES, AND PAST OR EXISTING OPERATIONS

1 Analyze the structure below so that you can reproduce it from memory on a separate sheet of paper. Make use of a structure analysis diagram.

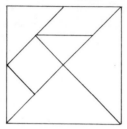

2 Analyze the operation pictured below so that you can describe it from memory on a separate sheet of paper. Then draw a picture of the figure which should come after number eight. Make use of a phase analysis diagram.

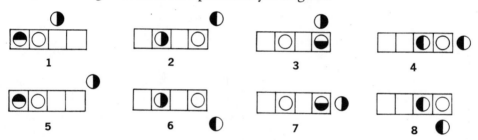

3 Analyze the objects pictured below so that you can name them from memory on a separate sheet of paper. Make use of a classification diagram.

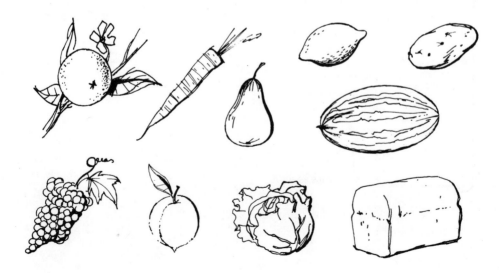

4 Analyze the structure below so that you can reproduce it from memory on a separate sheet of paper. Make use of a structure analysis diagram.

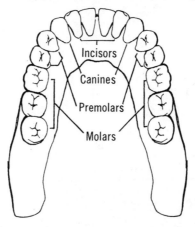

5 Analyze the passage below so that you can reproduce its meaning from memory on a separate sheet of paper. Make use of an operation analysis diagram.

HAMLET: To what base uses we may return, Horatio! Why may not imagination trace the noble dust of Alexander till 'a find it stopping a bunghole?

HORATIO: 'Twere to consider too curiously, to consider so.

HAMLET: No, faith, not a jot, but to follow him thither with modesty enough, and likelihood to lead it; as thus: Alexander died, Alexander was buried, Alexander returneth to dust; the dust is earth; of earth we make loam; and why of that loam whereto he was converted might they not stop a beer barrel?

> Imperious Caesar, dead and turned to clay,
> Might stop a hole to keep the wind away.
> O, that that earth which kept the world in awe
> Should patch a wall t' expel the winter's flaw!

Shakespeare, *Hamlet,* V, i, 190-203.

6 Analyze the passage below so that you can reproduce from memory its meaning on a separate sheet of paper. Make use of a classification diagram.

All states, all powers, that have held and hold rule over men have been and are either republics or principalities.

Principalities are either hereditary, in which the family has been long established; or they are new.

The new are either entirely new, as was Milan to Francesco Sforza, or they are, as it were, members annexed to the hereditary state of the prince who has acquired them, as was the kingdom of Naples to that of the King of Spain.

Such dominions thus acquired are either accustomed to live under a prince, or to live in freedom; and are acquired either by the arms of the prince himself, or of others, or else by fortune or by ability.

Machiavelli, *The Prince,* in *Great Books of the Western World,* XXIII, p. 3.

7 Analyze the map below so that you can reproduce it from memory on a separate sheet of paper. Make use of a structure analysis diagram.

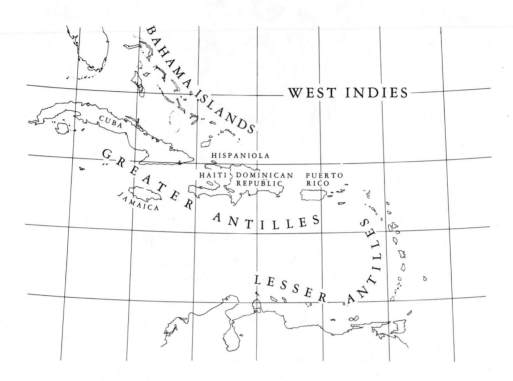

8 Analyze the sequence below so that you can reproduce it, together with the three numbers which should come next in the series, from memory on a separate sheet of paper. Make use of an operation analysis diagram.

4, 9, 13, 14, 18, 20, 34, 41, 47, 50, 62, 68, 86, 95, 103,

108, 128, 138, 160, 171, 181, 188, 216, 230, 256, 269, 281,

290, 326, 344, 374, 389, 403, 414, _____, _____, _____

9 Analyze the objects pictured below so that you can name them from memory on a separate sheet of paper. Make use of a classification diagram.

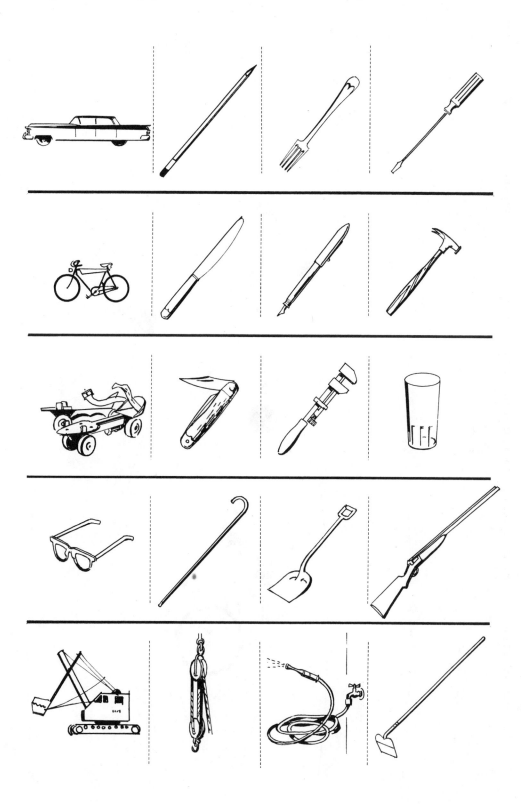

Analyze the representation of the solar system below so that you can reproduce it from memory on a separate sheet of paper. Make use of a structure analysis diagram.

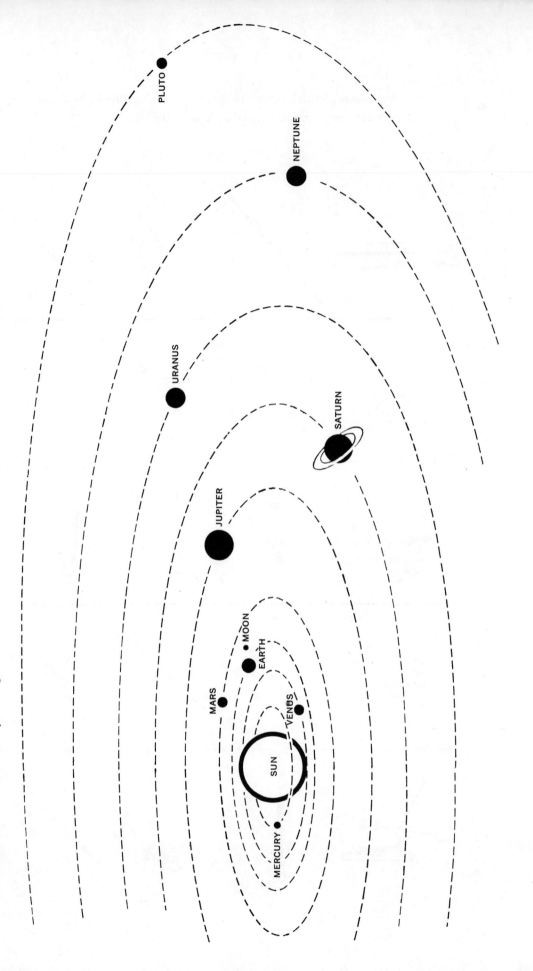

11 Analyze the quotation below so that you can reproduce its meaning from memory on a separate sheet of paper. Make use of an operation analysis diagram.

IN the beginning God created the heaven and the earth. And the earth was without form, and void; and darkness *was* upon the face of the deep. And the Spirit of God moved upon the face of the waters. And God said, Let there be light: and there was light. And God saw the light, that *it was* good: and God divided the light from the darkness. And God called the light Day, and the darkness he called Night. And the evening and the morning were the first day.

And God said, Let there be a firmament in the midst of the waters, and let it divide the waters from the waters. And God made the firmament and divided the waters which *were* under the firmament from the waters which *were* above the firmament: and it was so. And God called the firmament Heaven. And the evening and the morning were the second day.

And God said, Let the waters under the heaven be gathered together unto one place, and let the dry *land* appear: and it was so. And God called the dry *land* Earth; and the gathering together of the waters called he Seas: and God saw that *it was* good. And God said, Let the earth bring forth grass, the herb yielding seed, *and* the fruit tree yielding fruit after his kind, whose seed *is* in itself, upon the earth: and it was so. And the earth brought forth grass, *and* herb yielding seed after his kind, and the tree yielding fruit, whose seed *was* in itself, after his kind: and God saw that *it was* good. And the evening and the morning were the third day.

And God said, Let there be lights in the firmament of the heaven to divide the day from the night; and let them be for signs, and for seasons, and for days, and years: and let them be for lights in the firmament of the heaven to give light upon the earth: and it was so. And God made two great lights; the greater light to rule the day, and the lesser light to rule the night: *he made* the stars also. And God set them in the firmament of the heaven to give light upon the earth, and to rule over the day and over the night, and to divide the light from the darkness: and God saw that *it was* good. And the evening and the morning were the fourth day. And God said, Let the waters bring forth abundantly the moving creature that hath life, and fowl *that* may fly above the earth in the open firmament of heaven. And God created great whales, and every living creature that moveth, which the waters brought forth abundantly, after their kind, and every winged fowl after his kind: and God saw that *it was* good. And God blessed them, saying, Be fruitful, and multiply, and fill the waters in the seas, and let fowl multiply in the earth. And the evening and the morning were the fifth day.

And God said, Let the earth bring forth the living creature after his kind, cattle, and creeping thing, and beast of the earth after his kind: and it was so. And God made the beast of the earth after his kind, and cattle after their kind, and everything that creepeth upon the earth after his kind: and God saw that *it was* good.

And God said, Let us make man in our image, after our likeness: and let them have dominion over the fish of the sea, and over the fowl of the air, and over the cattle, and over all the earth, and over every creeping thing that creepeth upon the earth. So God created man in his *own* image, in the image of God created he him; male and female created he them. And God blessed them, and God said unto them, Be fruitful, and multiply, and replenish the earth, and subdue it: and have dominion over the fish of the sea, and over the fowl of the air, and over every living thing that moveth upon the earth.

And God said, Behold, I have given you every herb bearing seed, which *is* upon the face of all the earth, and every tree, in the which *is* the fruit of a tree yielding seed; to you it shall be for meat. And to every beast of the earth, and to every fowl of the air, and to every thing that creepeth upon the earth, wherein *there is* life, *I have given* every green herb for meat: and it was so. And God saw every thing that he had made, and, behold, *it was* very good. And the evening and the morning were the sixth day.

THUS the heavens and the earth were finished, and all the host of them. And on the seventh day God ended his work which he had made; and he rested on the seventh day from all his work which he had made. And God blessed the seventh day, and sanctified it: because that in it he had rested from all his work which God created and made.

Genesis 1:1-31 and 2:1-3.

12 Analyze the passage below so that you can reproduce its meaning from memory on a separate sheet of paper. Make use of a classification diagram.

Expressions which are in no way composite signify substance, quantity, quality, relation, place, time, position, state, action, or affection. To sketch my meaning roughly, examples of substance are 'man' or 'the horse', of quantity, such terms as 'two cubits long' or 'three cubits long', of quality, such attributes as 'white', 'grammatical'. 'Double', 'half', 'greater', fall under the category of relation; 'in the market place', 'in the Lyceum', under that of place; 'yesterday', 'last year', under that of time. 'Lying', 'sitting', are terms indicating position, 'shod', 'armed', state; 'to lance', 'to cauterize', action; 'to be lanced', 'to be cauterized', affection.

Aristotle, *Categories,* in *Great Books of the Western World,* VIII, pp. 5-6.

3*5*3

WORKING CLASSIFICATION, ANALYSIS OF PLANNED STRUCTURES, AND ANALYSIS OF PLANNED OPERATIONS

1. Make a working classification of automobiles, involving at least four vertical sorting factors.

2. Plan a rearrangement of the books of your personal library. Make use of a structure analysis diagram of at least four terms.

3. Make a plan for an actual or hypothetical speech. Make use of an operation analysis diagram of at least seven terms.

4. Make a working classification, involving at least seven vertical sorting factors, of the possible causes of war.

5. Make a plan for the rearrangement of furniture in a room of your home. Make use of a structure analysis diagram of at least nine terms.

6. Create a new dance step, making use of a phase analysis diagram of at least twelve terms.

7. Make a working classification, involving at least fifteen vertical sorting factors, of the ways fires may get started in the home.

8. Design a garment, such as a blouse, shirt, or coat. Make use of a structure analysis diagram of at least eight terms.

9. Plan an actual or hypothetical social event involving a number of phases. Make use of a phase analysis diagram of at least twenty terms.

10. Make a working classification, involving at least eighteen vertical sorting factors, of all possible subjects of conversation.

11. Design a chair unlike any you have seen before. Make use of a structure analysis diagram of at least fifteen terms.

12. Make an outline for a book which you would like to write. Your outline, which will be an operation analysis, should involve at least twenty-five terms.

13. Make a working classification, involving at least twenty vertical sorting factors, of the goals which act as motives for your action.

14. Make a sketch for an abstract painting of your own design. Accompany the sketch with a structure analysis diagram of at least eighteen terms.

15. Plan a complex operation, such as a business venture, in which phases are a relevant consideration. Use a phase analysis diagram of at least thirty terms.

SEMANTIC GROWTH

TEXT

Semantic growth is the process by which old words take on new senses — that is, become ambiguous. There are seven sorts of semantic growths:

SIMILITUDES (SENSORY, AFFECTIVE, and LOGICAL)
IRONIES
ABSTRACT-CONCRETIONS
GENUS-SPECIES
STRUCTURALS
OPERATIONALS
METAPHORS (*proportional* metaphors)

Examples will be given of six of the seven kinds of semantic growths; metaphors will be dealt with separately in Section Five. It should be clearly understood throughout this section that we are not concerned with the actual semantic history of any particular word. We *assume* the "old" and "new" senses given regardless of their historical development, which may or may not be known. We are interested in how words *do* grow (in the mind) rather than how they *have* grown "historically."

A similitude is a name which has been transferred to a thing or quality because it refers to a similar thing or quality. There are sensory, affective, and logical similitudes. Sensory similitudes involve experiences of vision, hearing, taste, smell, and other sensations. We notice that the sound of an engine resembles the roar of a lion so we say that the engine "roars." *Roar* is a sensory similitude involving hearing. The old sense of *roar* is "the deep rumbling sound of a lion or another such animal." The new sense of *roar* is "the loud noise made by the operation of an engine." The word *roar* takes on a new meaning — becomes ambiguous or increasingly ambiguous. We notice that the flap beneath the laces of a shoe resembles a dog's tongue so we speak of the "tongue" of a shoe. *Tongue* is a sensory similitude involving sight, for by the use of our eyes we *see* that the tongue of a shoe resembles the tongue of a dog. By virtue of the visual resemblance between the two objects the name of one is transferred to the other and the word *tongue* takes on an additional meaning. A sensory similitude is a name which has been transferred from one thing or quality to another because of a sensory (or perceptual) resemblance between the two.

An affective similitude is a name which has been transferred to a thing or quality because it refers to an emotionally similar thing or quality. Affective similitudes involve emotional qualities such as love, fear, anger, beauty, disgust, happiness, and awe. A pretty girl is called a "flower" of womanhood because she is beautiful like a flower; a pretty girl and a flower are similar in the esthetic emotion of beauty. An offensive person is called a "skunk" because he is repugnant like a skunk; an offensive person and a skunk are alike in respect of the emotion of disgust. *Flower* and *skunk* become the names for a pretty girl and an offensive person, respectively, because these people resemble emotionally a beautiful flower and an offensive skunk, in the old senses of the words.

A logical similitude is a name which has been transferred from one thing or quality to another thing or quality because both have a similar *relationship* to a *third* thing or quality. Logical similitudes are called logical because they involve a similarity between *relationships*. In the sentence, "Aunt Sophie is the maid of the family," *maid* is a logical similitude. The old sense of *maid* is "female servant." The new sense of *maid* is "Aunt Sophie." Aunt Sophie is called a maid because she performs the same household duties for the family that a maid would perform. Aunt Sophie does not necessarily look like a maid and she does not necessarily arouse the same emotions which a maid might arouse, but she is *related to the family* in the same way in which a maid might be related to the family; indeed, one might say, "Uncle Ernest is the maid in our family." Logical similitudes may be expressed as the proportion A is to B as C is to B or $A/B = C/B$. A maid (A) might be related to the family (B) in the same way that Aunt Sophie (C) is related to the family (B). The name of A is transferred to C because both have the same relationship to B.

IRONIES

While similitudes have to do with similarities between things or qualities, ironies have to do with differences between things or qualities. An irony is a name of a thing or quality which has been transferred to an *opposite* thing or quality. A statement of obvious fact may be greeted with the comment, "Amazing!" The word *amazing* is a semantic growth expressing an ironic relationship. The old sense of *amazing* is "astonishing, surprising." The new sense of *amazing* is "*not* astonishing or surprising." The new sense of *amazing* is the opposite of the old sense. If we call an old man a "youngster," we are being ironic. The old sense of *youngster* is "child." The new sense of *youngster* is "old man." In respect of age an old man is the opposite of a child. An irony is a name which has been transferred from one thing or quality to an opposite thing or quality.

ABSTRACT-CONCRETIONS

Similitudes and ironies have to do with similarities or differences between things or between qualities. Abstractions and concretions, however, are concerned with things *and* their qualities. An abstraction is a name which has been transferred from a thing to one of its qualities. A concretion is a name which has been transferred from a quality of a thing to the thing itself. We notice that oranges have a characteristic color so we transfer the name of the fruit to the color of the fruit and speak of "orange" objects. The name of a concrete thing, a citrus fruit, is transferred to an abstract thing, a color. *Orange* is an abstraction because it is transferred from a concrete to an abstract thing. We notice that soldiers dress in a uniform way so we speak of their "uniforms." *Uniform* is a concretion because the name of the abstract quality of uniformity is transferred to a suit of clothes which possesses the quality of uniformity. Abstractions go from the concrete to the abstract; concretions go from the abstract to the concrete.

GENUS-SPECIES

There are three sorts of semantic growths involving analytic relationships: genus-species, structurals, and operationals. There are two sorts of genus-species word growths: generalizations and specializations. A generalization is a name which has been transferred from a specific class to a more inclusive class. A specialization is a name which has been transferred from a general class to a particular subclass within the general class. Let us assume that the old sense of *fish* is "any cold-blooded animal with a backbone and gills which lives in water." According to this definition crabs and whales are not fish. Crabs do not have backbones and whales are warm-blooded. If we wish to have a name for all creatures which live permanently in water, we may select the name of the particular water animal most familiar to us, *fish*. Thus if we speak of crabs and whales as "fish," we have developed a new sense of the word *fish* by the process of generalization, making the new sense of *fish* more general than the old sense. "Fish" in the old sense of the word are one species of "fish" in the new sense of the word. *Fish* is a generalization because it has been transferred from a specific class to a more general class.

Let us assume that the old sense of *plant* is that expressed in the sentence, "Trees, shrubs, flowers, and vines are plants." If we use *plant* in a more specific sense, as in the sentence, "We have plants in our yard but no trees," we have developed a new sense of the word *plant* by the process of specialization. The new sense of *plant* is more specific than the old sense. The new sense of *plant* is "any soft-stemmed member of the plant kingdom, as distinguished from a shrub or tree" while the old sense of *plant* is "any form of life incapable of voluntary movement; as any tree, shrub, or weed." A "plant" in the new sense is a *kind* of plant in the old sense. *Plant* is a specialization because it has taken on a more specific meaning. Generalizations and specializations involve the genus-species relationship. A species is a kind of its genus; a genus includes two or more species. A generalization is a name which has been transferred from a species to its genus; a specialization is a name which has been transferred from a genus to one of its species.

STRUCTURALS

Structurals are a second kind of analytic word growth. While generalizations and specializations involve the relationship of a species to its genus, structurals involve the relationship of a part to its whole. A woman is a *kind* of man but a leg is a *part* of a man. A structural is a name which has been transferred from a part to a whole or from a whole to a part. Let us assume that the old sense of *flower* is "blossom of a plant." If we speak of a "flower" as an entire flowering plant, complete with leaves, stem, and roots, we have developed a new sense of the word *flower* by the process of structure analysis. The old sense of *flower* is "blossom." The new sense of *flower* is "flowering plant." A "flower" (blossom) is a part of an entire "flower." *Flower* is a part-to-whole structural because the name of a part has been transferred to a whole. By the reverse process we may take *almond,* the name of the tree, and let it mean "almond," the fruit of the tree. The old sense of *almond* is "almond tree" while the new sense of *almond* is "fruit of an almond tree." The new sense signifies a part of the structure signified by the old sense. An "almond" (the fruit) is a part of an "almond" (the tree). *Almond* is a whole-to-part structural because the name of a whole has been transferred to a part of the whole.

OPERATIONALS

Operationals are a third kind of analytic word growth. An operation is a changing structure. Thus in operation analysis we have need of the terminology of structure analysis as well as the terminology of change. We have need of the terms *structure* (synonym for *whole)* and *part* as well as the terms *operation, stage, phase, juncture, function,* and *purpose.* But in studying operational *semantic growths* we have no need to consider directly the names of junctures, functions, and purposes. Functions and purposes are generally abstract concepts and semantic shifts involving their names usually fall into the category of abstract-concretions. If we call fire *heat* after its function of providing warmth, we have developed not an operational but a concretion, for "heat," in the old sense of the word, is a quality of fire as well as a function. Although junctures are useful division points between stages, their names tend to "expand" them into small stages. Although a sunset may be thought of as a juncture, the word *sunset* generally denotes a stage — something requiring time, however little. It is expedient, therefore, in studying operational semantic growths to consider that junctures are small stages. Thus the following "things" may be involved in operational sense growths:

> an operation
> stages
> a structure *(the changing structure of the operation)*
> parts
> phases

An operational semantic growth occurs whenever, in the context of an operation, the name of one of the elements listed above is transferred to another.

Let us assume that the old sense of *safari* is "hunting expedition, usually in Africa." If we call the caravan which makes such an expedition a "safari," we have developed a new sense of *safari* by operation analysis. A safari, in the old sense of the word, is the operation of a hunting expedition. The structure of the operation consists of the caravan, the terrain, and the game—that is, the environment, the hunters, the bearers, and their equipment. Operation Safari consists of the interaction of the caravan with its environment, but *safari* in its new sense pertains only to the caravan. The caravan is a part of the total structure which, as it changes, is the operation. The name of the total operation of the hunting expedition is transferred to the caravan, a part of the total structure which undergoes change. *Safari* is an operation-to-part operational because the name of an operation is transferred to a part of the structure of the operation. Thus we may say, "The safari is on safari."

Let us assume that the old sense of *eating* is "chewing and swallowing" and that the new sense is that expressed in the sentence, "He is eating dinner." In its new sense *eating* refers to the total process involved in consuming a meal, including drinking, lifting one's fork, and passing the butter. Chewing and swallowing is a single stage in the total operation. The name of this single stage is transferred to the integral operation of consuming a meal. *Eating* is a stage-to-operation operational because the name of a stage is transferred to the operation which contains it. Operational word growths occur when, in the context of an operation, the name of a stage, operation, structure, part, or phase is transferred to another such component.

EXERCISES

PICTURED EXERCISES

Eight pairs of things are indicated below. On the line to the left of each pair write the word from the list provided which may be applied to both things. Then, imagining that the name of one thing has been transferred to the other, indicate on the line to the right whether the semantic growth is a sensory similitude, affective similitude, logical similitude, irony, abstract-concretion, genus-species, structural, or operational.

A. Sweet   B. Portable   C. Baseball   D. Duck   E. Cog   F. Cats   G. Spear   H. Ferocious

Words   *Semantic growths*

1_____

2_____

3_____

4_____

5_____

6_____

7_____

8_____

4*2*2

CLASSIFICATION EXERCISE

Write the sorting factors on the appropriate lines of the diagram below and put the letters of the specimens in the appropriate pigeonholes.

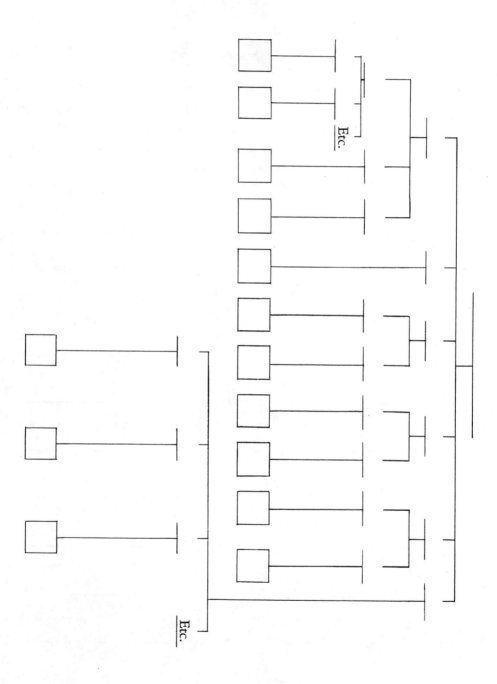

1. Part-to-operation	12. Visual
2. Similitude	13. Operation-to-phase
3. Irony	14. Genus-species
4. Sensory	15. Abstraction
5. Part-to-whole	16. Semantic growths
6. Stage-to-part	17. Concretion
7. Abstract-concrete	18. Auditory
8. Generalization	19. Whole-to-part
9. Affective	20. Structural
10. Specialization	21. Logical
11. Operational	

SPECIMENS:

a. OLD SENSE: This *bed* is soft.
NEW SENSE: The hard ground was his *bed* for the night.

b. OS: The center hiked the *football* to the quarterback.
NS: *Football* is a rugged game.

c. OS: People used to drink out of *dippers.*
NS: The Big *Dipper* is part of the constellation of Ursa Major.

d. OS: He's a musician, not an *artist.*
NS: A poet is an *artist.*

e. OS: We arrived just after the first *dance.*
NS: Thank you for the *dance.*

f. OS: Take the *rubbish* to the dump.
NS: The *Gazette* is *rubbish.*

g. OS: The Allies *liberated* Belgium from the Germans.
NS: Hitler did his best to *liberate* England.

h. OS: He walked with slow, hesitant *steps.*
NS: He climbed the *steps* quickly.

i. OS: I heard a mouse *squeak.*
NS: My new shoes *squeak.*

j. OS: A *bat* is any heavy stick or club.
NS: A *bat* is a club used in baseball.

k. OS: Candy is *sweet.*
NS: Have a *sweet.*

l. OS: The human *ear* is composed of the external ear, the middle ear, and the inner ear.
NS: He has a cauliflower *ear.*

m. OS: She wore a *violet* in her hair.
NS: She wore *violet* stockings.

n. OS: The *earth* was wet with dew this morning.
NS: The *earth* is larger than Mars.

4*2*3

IDENTIFICATION OF SEMANTIC GROWTHS

Identify the semantic growth in each exercise below. The main purpose of this section is to sharpen the mind's awareness of useful shifts in meaning. Consequently semantic growths have been included in proportion to the useful mental discipline required to comprehend them. Similitudes, genus-species, and operationals have been included in greater numbers than abstract-concretions and structurals. Ironies have not been included at all. By a change of voice or other signs any word can be made to mean its opposite. This simple avenue of semantic change deserves recognition but extensive exercises to comprehend it are unnecessary.

You should go to great detail in identifying each semantic growth. If it is a similitude indicate whether it is sensory, affective, or logical. If it is a sensory similitude indicate whether it pertains to vision, hearing, or another sensory modality. If it involves the abstract-concrete relation indicate whether it is an abstraction or a concretion. If it is a genus-species semantic growth indicate whether it is a generalization or specialization. If it is a structural indicate whether the shift in sense involves a part-to-whole or whole-to-part relation. If it is an operational indicate whether the word, in each of its two senses, refers to a stage, an operation, a part, a structure, or a phase. You might consider making a classification diagram and pigeonholing each semantic growth as you identify it.

1. OLD SENSE: The Indian shot an *arrow* at a deer.

   NEW SENSE: An *arrow* on the wall pointed to the exit.

   SEMANTIC GROWTH_____

2. OS: An *artichoke* is a thistle-like plant with an edible head.

   NS: *Artichokes* are often boiled and eaten with mayonnaise or butter.

   SG _____

3. OS: Some guns are *automatic* in their firing.
   NS: The policeman carried an *automatic*.
   SG _____

4. OS: Babies *babble*.
   NS: Brooks *babble*.
   SG _____

5. OS: A *bean* is composed of a pod and seeds.
   NS: She was removing *beans* from their pods.
   SG _____

6. OS: Tar is *black*.
   NS: Everyone wore *black* to the funeral.
   SG _____

7. OS: The form had thirty-two *blanks*.
   NS: When he had answered all the questions, he returned the *blank* to the interviewer.
   SG _____

8. OS: The kerosene brought a sudden *blaze* to the fire.
   NS: The soldiers arrived amid a *blaze* of trumpets.
   SG _____

9. OS: The sky is *blue*.
   NS: The artist dabbed some *blue* onto the canvas.
   SG _____

10. OS: The water is *boiling*.
    NS: The eggs are *boiling*.
    SG _____

11. OS: He *bounced* the basketball and then shot a basket.
    NS: The little girl *bounced* the ball for ten minutes.
    SG _____

12. OS: Not all Indians are *brave*.
    NS: The settlers were attacked by *braves*.
    SG _____

13. OS: The *bullet* was embedded in the bone of his right calf.
    NS: "How many *bullets* does your automatic hold?"
    SG _____

14. OS: A *button* was missing from his shirt.
    NS: Daisies have yellow *buttons*.
    SG _____

15. OS: The bees were *buzzing*.
    NS: The alarm clock was *buzzing*.
    SG _____

16. OS: The *calf* was a Holstein.
    NS: The young of cows, walruses, and elephants are *calves*.
    SG _____

17. OS: My *camera* takes good pictures.
    NS: There are two sorts of *cameras*: photographic and television.
    SG _____

18. OS: A *cane* is a walking stick made from cane.
    NS: He had a plastic *cane*.
    SG _____

19. OS: Playing cards, calling cards, and business cards are sorts of *cards*.
    NS: The salesman left his *card*.
    SG _____

20. OS: There is a *cedar* in our
        back yard.
    NS: *Cedar* is the wood of a
        cedar tree.
    SG _____

21. OS: A *cell* is a small room, as
        in a prison, monastery, or
        hospital.
    NS: A *cell* is a room for a
        prison inmate.
    SG _____

22. OS: Albert is the *center* on
        our football team.
    NS: Albert is going to *center*
        the football.
    SG _____

23. OS: A *century* is any period of
        one hundred years.
    NS: We are living in the
        twentieth *century*.
    SG _____

24. OS: *China* is an oriental
        country.
    NS: *China* is made of kaolin.
    SG _____

25. OS: The hens were *chuckling*.
    NS: He was *chuckling* at the
        cartoons.
    SG _____

26. OS: The *church* is a fine
        structure.
    NS: *Church* lasted for an hour.
    SG _____

27. OS: The *city* of New York has
        many skyscrapers and
        interesting people.
    NS: A majority of the *city*
        voted for the school bond
        issue.
    SG _____

28. OS: *Class* was over at 3:30.
    NS: The *class* started in
        September and ended in
        June.
    SG _____

29. OS: "What *color* is the paint?"
    NS: The artist scraped the
        colors from his palette.
    SG _____

30. OS: They left the stadium
        before the *competition*
        was over.
    NS: The *competition* arrived
        by bus.
    SG _____

31. OS: Water becomes *concrete*
        when it is frozen.
    NS: The building was made of
        concrete and steel.
    SG _____

32. OS: *Copper* is used as an
        electrical conductor.
    NS: She has *copper* hair.
    SG _____

33. OS: A *corona* is a crown.
    NS: During a total eclipse the
        sun has a *corona*.
    SG _____

34. OS: Both the music and
        dancing of the *cotillion*
        were lively.
    NS: The orchestra was playing
        a *cotillion*.
    SG _____

35. OS: *Cotton* is a plant which
        grows in warm climates.
    NS: He separated the *cotton*
        from the seeds.
    SG _____

36. os: He didn't bother to *countersink* the screws.
NS: He lost the *countersink*.
SG _____

37. os: A *creature* is anything, animate or inanimate, thought of as created by God.
NS: A *creature* is a living being, a man or an animal.
SG _____

38. os: Men and animals are *creatures*.
NS: Men are not *creatures* but immortal beings.
SG _____

39. os: His *criticism* was mostly favorable.
NS: He followed his *criticism* with a compliment.
SG _____

40. os: The *crow's feet* were large.
NS: Her eyes have *crow's-feet*.
SG _____

41. os: He *cut* himself with a knife.
NS: She *cut* him with a sarcastic remark.
SG _____

42. os: He *cut* his hand.
NS: He put a bandage over the *cut*.
SG _____

43. os: The night was *dark*.
NS: What *dark* deed could he be planning?
SG _____

44. os: A *day* is twenty-four hours long.
NS: Night follows *day*.
SG _____

45. os: His *death* occurred on the night of the 27th.
NS: Is *death* a state of nothingness or a state of existence?
SG _____

46. os: A *decision* is an act of deciding.
NS: He would not alter his *decision*.
SG _____

47. os: A *delta* is a letter of the Greek alphabet.
NS: There was a *delta* at the mouth of the river.
SG _____

48. os: This desert is a *desolate* place.
NS: The old woman's face had a *desolate* look.
SG _____

49. os: "Would you like to *drive?*"
NS: He went for a *drive* in the country.
SG _____

50. os: New York is *east* of California.
NS: She went to college in the *East*.
SG _____

51. os: Reptiles, birds, and fish lay *eggs*.
NS: She bought some *eggs* and bacon at the grocery store.
SG _____

52. os: *Eyes* are organs of sight.
NS: A German shepherd was the blind man's *eyes*.
SG _____

53. OS: The eagle lost a *feather*.
    NS: The periscope made a foamy *feather* on the ocean's surface.
    SG _____

54. OS: *Fire* is hot.
    NS: He is on *fire* with fever.
    SG _____

55. OS: She mopped the *floor*.
    NS: He works on the fourth *floor*.
    SG _____

56. OS: It was the co-pilot's turn to *fly* the airplane.
    NS: Every member of the crew helps *fly* an airplane.
    SG _____

57. OS: The plow made *furrows* in the ground.
    NS: There were *furrows* in the fisherman's brow.
    SG _____

58. OS: A *glass* is a drinking utensil made of glass.
    NS: This is a plastic *glass*.
    SG _____

59. OS: This is a *glass* skillet.
    NS: A *glass* is a drinking utensil made of glass.
    SG _____

60. OS: Caves are *gloomy* places.
    NS: "Why are you so *gloomy?*"
    SG _____

61. OS: He cut his *hand*.
    NS: All *hands* were on deck.
    SG _____

62. OS: To *hang* is to suspend by means of a rope, chain, string, or other connection.
    NS: "When are they going to *hang* the murderer?"
    SG _____

63. OS: The coffin was carried to the grave on a wooden *hearse*.
    NS: The *hearse* led the funeral procession through heavy traffic.
    SG _____

64. OS: The sidewalk is *icy*.
    NS: She gave him an *icy* stare.
    SG _____

65. OS: An *igloo* is an Eskimo dwelling.
    NS: "Turn on the heater; this house is an *igloo*."
    SG _____

66. OS: A *jet* is a stream of gas which propels a jet aircraft.
    NS: The *jet* landed safely.
    SG _____

67. OS: A *joint* is a place of contact between two or more bones in a human being or animal.
    NS: A *joint* is any connection between two or more parts of a structure.
    SG _____

68. OS: A *judge* is any person who judges, as in a contest or trial.
    NS: The court stood as the *judge* took his place at the bench.
    SG _____

69. OS: A *leech* is a worm formerly used by physicians to bleed patients.
    NS: A *leech* is a mechanical device used in medicine to draw blood from patients.
    SG _____

70. OS: He has a pain in his *leg*.
    NS: He has a wooden *leg*.
    SG _____

71. OS: A *lemon* is a citrus fruit.
    NS: Her dress was *lemon* and pink.
    SG _____

72. OS: *Lettuce* is the basic ingredient of most salads.
    NS: It takes a lot of *lettuce* to join a country club.
    SG _____

73. OS: The *moon* is the earth's natural satellite.
    NS: Mars has two *moons*.
    SG _____

74. OS: She tried to *mount* the horse.
    NS: Her *mount* was frisky.
    SG _____

75. OS: *Mules* were once used to pull boats along canals.
    NS: A *mule* is a tractor or other machine used to pull boats through canals.
    SG _____

76. OS: I enjoyed the *music* but I didn't care for the singing.
    NS: Light opera is lovely *music*.
    SG _____

77. OS: The bird flew to its *nest*.
    NS: Birds, insects, and reptiles have *nests*.
    SG _____

78. OS: A *nucleus* is the central part of a thing.
    NS: The electrons were stripped from their *nucleus*.
    SG _____

79. OS: An *oar* is an implement used for rowing.
    NS: One of the *oars* on the galley died of scurvy.
    SG _____

80. OS: Over two-thirds of the earth's surface is covered by the *ocean*.
    NS: California borders the Pacific *Ocean*.
    SG _____

81. OS: The *oxbow* was put around the neck of the ox.
    NS: The rapids were a mile south of the *oxbow*.
    SG _____

82. OS: Mary's *parents* are divorced.
    NS: A *parent* is an organism which has produced other organisms.
    SG _____

83. OS: Her *perfume* filled the room.
    NS: The air was sweet with the *perfume* of flowers.
    SG _____

84. OS: "Are you going to *photograph* the temple?"
    NS: "Do you have a *photograph* of her?"
    SG _____

85. OS: The needle *pierced* his arm.
    NS: A sudden pain *pierced* his chest as he coughed.
    SG _____

86. OS: The moon, the sun, and Mars are *planets*.
    NS: A moon is a satellite of a *planet*.
    SG _____

87. OS: The *process* of photosynthesis is an interesting one.
    NS: The surgeon removed the abnormal *process* from the patient's brain.
    SG _____

88. OS: The rope was wedged between the *pulley* and the frame.
    NS: They lifted the engine with a compound *pulley*.
    SG _____

89. OS: A *pygmy* is a member of any of a number of races of dwarfs.
    NS: A *pygmy* is an abnormally small human being, animal, or plant.
    SG _____

90. OS: It was a *radiant* spring morning.
    NS: She gave him a *radiant* smile.
    SG _____

91. OS: She felt the *rain* against her face.
    NS: The *rain* lasted until midnight.
    SG _____

92. OS: They have a gas *refrigerator*.
    NS: The Arctic was a natural *refrigerator* for their provisions.
    SG _____

93. OS: This horse isn't used to a *saddle*.
    NS: The mountain climber crossed the *saddle* between the two summits.
    SG _____

94. OS: This *sail* needs mending.
    NS: He took his yacht for a *sail* in the Atlantic.
    SG _____

95. OS: "Please pass the *salt*."
    NS: Sodium chloride is one type of *salt*.
    SG _____

96. OS: The kitten drank its milk from a *saucer*.
    NS: The spaceman landed his *saucer* in a field of corn.
    SG _____

97. OS: He was sanding the *seat* of the chair.
    NS: "Pull up a *seat*."
    SG _____

98. OS: This dress is made of *silk*.
    NS: She didn't remove all the *silk* from the corn.
    SG _____

99. OS: The tires *skidded*.
    NS: The car *skidded*.
    SG _____

100. OS: Ice is *solid* water.
     NS: Copper is a *solid* at room temperature.
     SG _____

101. OS: Horses swat flies with their *tails*.
     NS: "Look at the *tail* of that comet."
     SG _____

102. OS: The *tedder* wiped the perspiration from his brow.
    NS: The *tedder* was in the shop for repairs.
    SG _____

103. OS: The *test* was over at 3:00.
    NS: "Turn in your *tests,* please."
    SG _____

104. OS: Happiness is an experience, not a *thing.*
    NS: Qualities are abstract *things.*
    SG _____

105. OS: She was *toasting* marshmallows in the fire.
    NS: He was *toasting* his feet by the fire.
    SG _____

106. OS: The locomotive was separated from the *train.*
    NS: The *train* is late.
    SG _____

107. OS: To *utter* is to communicate vocally.
    NS: To *utter* is to communicate in any way, whether in speech or writing.
    SG _____

108. OS: A sea anemone is an animal, not a *vegetable.*
    NS: A tomato is a *vegetable,* not a fruit.
    SG _____

109. OS: Rats, maggots, lice and other such animals are *vermin.*
    NS: "I'll move before I have those *vermin* for neighbors."
    SG _____

110. OS: A *watch* is a candle divided into segments which when burned measure the passage of time.
    NS: Her *watch* is self-winding.
    SG _____

111. OS: The *waves* were breaking on the rocks.
    NS: The barber cut the *wave* from his hair.
    SG _____

112. OS: The child was *whirling* in a circle.
    NS: The drunk man's head was *whirling.*
    SG _____

113. OS: He *whispered* into her ear.
    NS: The breeze *whispered* through the pines.
    SG _____

114. OS: She is *winking* at him.
    NS: The red lights at the railroad crossing are *winking* on and off.
    SG _____

115. OS: He cut the insulation from the *wire.*
    NS: The telephone *wires* are down.
    SG _____

116. OS: The *world* circles the sun once a year.
    NS: Our solar system is only a small part of the *world,* which may be infinite.
    SG _____

117. OS: "Are *X-rays* harmful?"
    NS: The doctor studied the *X-rays* of the child's arm.
    SG _____

4*2*4

DISCOVERY AND CREATION OF SEMANTIC GROWTHS

Discover or create in your own mind the following:

TEN SENSORY SIMILITUDES

FIVE AFFECTIVE SIMILITUDES

THREE LOGICAL SIMILITUDES

FIVE IRONIES

FIVE ABSTRACTIONS

FIVE CONCRETIONS

FIVE GENERALIZATIONS

FIVE SPECIALIZATIONS

TEN STRUCTURALS

TEN OPERATIONALS

Record them on a separate sheet of paper. It may be helpful to consult books, magazines, and the dictionary and to observe objects and activities in the world about you, considering why they and their elements have the names they do.

*   *   *   *   *

ANALOGIES

SECTION 5

PROPORTIONAL ANALOGIES

TEXT

When we write *one is to two*, or *one over two*, or *one to two*, or *1/2*, or *1:2*, we are thinking of a ratio or relation between one and two of the sort that makes up fractions in arithmetic. If we say that one is to two as three is to six and write *1/2 = 3/6*, or *1:2::3:6*, we call the comparison a proportion or proportional analogy. But we don't have to stick to numbers. We may say that a dog is to a pup as a bear is to a cub or a cat to a kitten and still have a proportional analogy; in fact, you can say that a whelk shell is to a hermit crab as a hut is to a hermit. Let us just say at this point that as long as the *relation* between any *a* and *b* strikes you as similar to the *relation* between some *c* and *d*, you have a proportional analogy.

5*1*2

EXERCISES

5*1*2*1

VERBAL ANALOGIES

In each exercise fill in the blank with the word which makes the two sides of the proportion similar in their relationships.

The sample exercise below has been worked for you.

$$\frac{\text{red}}{\text{blood}} = \frac{\textit{green}}{\text{grass}} \qquad \text{/bitter, black, green, wet}$$

Red is related to blood in the same way that green is related to grass. Green is the color of grass just as red is the color of blood. The two sides of the proportion are similar because they both express the relationship of a color to its object.

1. $\dfrac{\text{sour}}{\text{lemon}} = \dfrac{\text{sweet}}{\rule{2cm}{0.4pt}}$ /hot, candy, salt, delicious

2. $\dfrac{\text{feather}}{\text{bird}} = \dfrac{\text{scale}}{\rule{2cm}{0.4pt}}$ /fish, fin, animal, man

3. $\dfrac{\text{bird}}{\text{flying}} = \dfrac{\rule{2cm}{0.4pt}}{\text{swimming}}$ /gills, fish, ocean, boat

4. $\dfrac{\text{blue}}{\text{color}} = \dfrac{\text{sweet}}{\rule{2cm}{0.4pt}}$ /sour, mouth, fig, taste

5. $\dfrac{\text{covers}}{\text{book}} = \dfrac{\rule{2cm}{0.4pt}}{\text{person}}$ /head, clothes, man, nose

6. $\dfrac{\rule{2cm}{0.4pt}}{\text{honesty}} = \dfrac{\text{emotion}}{\text{love}}$ /falsehood, passion, witness, virtue

7. $\dfrac{\text{card game}}{\text{dealing}} = \dfrac{\text{dinner}}{\rule{2cm}{0.4pt}}$ /serving, eating, chewing, washing dishes

8. $\dfrac{\text{man}}{\rule{2cm}{0.4pt}} = \dfrac{\text{bird}}{\text{beak}}$ /head, mouth, body, leg

9. $\dfrac{\text{seven}}{\text{number}} = \dfrac{\text{large}}{\quad}$ /size, small, whale, distance

10. $\dfrac{\text{arrival}}{\text{departure}} = \dfrac{\quad}{\text{death}}$ /life, person, birth, train

11. $\dfrac{\text{elbow}}{\text{arm}} = \dfrac{\text{knee}}{\quad}$ /walking, finger, leg, nose

12. $\dfrac{\text{car}}{\text{road}} = \dfrac{\text{train}}{\quad}$ /track, vehicle, fast, wheel

13. $\dfrac{\text{baiting hook}}{\text{fishing}} = \dfrac{\quad}{\text{hunting}}$ /loading gun, firing gun, stalking game, aiming gun

14. $\dfrac{\text{violence}}{\text{activity}} = \dfrac{\text{melancholy}}{\quad}$ /evening, cruelty, mood, silence

15. $\dfrac{\text{man}}{\text{trousers}} = \dfrac{\text{woman}}{\quad}$ /clothing, skirt, hat, blanket

16. $\dfrac{\text{university}}{\text{institution}} = \dfrac{\text{mayor}}{\quad}$ /official, town, law, councilman

17. $\dfrac{\text{grass}}{\text{soil}} = \dfrac{\text{seaweed}}{\quad}$ /water, salty, river, fish

18. $\dfrac{\text{truthfulness}}{\text{court}} = \dfrac{\text{cleanliness}}{\quad}$ /virtue, restaurant, bath, pig

19. $\dfrac{\text{egg}}{\text{fish}} = \dfrac{\quad}{\text{plant}}$ /leaf, root, seed, stem

20. $\dfrac{\text{lion}}{\text{animal}} = \dfrac{\text{flower}}{\quad}$ /plant, grass, roots, rose

21. $\dfrac{\text{wave}}{\text{crest}} = \dfrac{\quad}{\text{peak}}$ /water, top, moving, mountain

22. $\dfrac{\text{falling}}{\text{gravitation}} = \dfrac{\text{collapse}}{\quad}$ /balloon, elasticity, pressure, destruction

23. $\dfrac{\text{professor}}{\quad} = \dfrac{\text{musician}}{\text{entertainment}}$ /pupils, school, homework, instruction

24. $\dfrac{\text{grains}}{\text{sand}} = \dfrac{\text{drops}}{\quad}$ /rain, snow, surf, flood

25. $\dfrac{\text{wave}}{\text{tide}} = \dfrac{\text{moment}}{\quad}$ /time, ocean, tardiness, clock

26. $\dfrac{\text{wife}}{\text{woman}} = \dfrac{\rule{2cm}{0.4pt}}{\text{man}}$ /father, groom, boy, husband

27. $\dfrac{\text{book}}{\rule{2cm}{0.4pt}} = \dfrac{\text{comb}}{\text{tooth}}$ /title, library, page, knowledge

28. $\dfrac{\text{boy}}{\text{child}} = \dfrac{\text{man}}{\rule{2cm}{0.4pt}}$ /father, uncle, adult, person

29. $\dfrac{\text{flower}}{\text{weed}} = \dfrac{\rule{2cm}{0.4pt}}{\text{crow}}$ /plant, swan, bird, buzzard

30. $\dfrac{\text{clock}}{\text{time}} = \dfrac{\rule{2cm}{0.4pt}}{\text{length}}$ /inch, scales, ruler, telescope

31. $\dfrac{\rule{2cm}{0.4pt}}{\text{hunting}} = \dfrac{\text{hook}}{\text{fishing}}$ /trigger, bullet, barrel, gun

32. $\dfrac{\text{clergyman}}{\text{priest}} = \dfrac{\text{doctor}}{\rule{2cm}{0.4pt}}$ /surgeon, nurse, hospital, lawyer

33. $\dfrac{\text{army}}{\text{soldier}} = \dfrac{\text{faculty}}{\rule{2cm}{0.4pt}}$ /school, education, students, teacher

34. $\dfrac{\rule{2cm}{0.4pt}}{\text{harvest}} = \dfrac{\text{landlord}}{\text{rent}}$ /farm, barn, cow, farmer

35. $\dfrac{\rule{2cm}{0.4pt}}{\text{assembling}} = \dfrac{\text{publishing}}{\text{binding}}$ /reading, book, advertising, manufacturing

36. $\dfrac{\text{secretary}}{\rule{2cm}{0.4pt}} = \dfrac{\text{teacher}}{\text{school}}$ /typewriter, office, dictation, desk

37. $\dfrac{\text{moon}}{\text{planet}} = \dfrac{\text{planet}}{\rule{2cm}{0.4pt}}$ /sun, space, galaxy, comet

38. $\dfrac{\text{spectator}}{\text{audience}} = \dfrac{\text{letter}}{\rule{2cm}{0.4pt}}$ /number, alphabet, sentence, pencil

39. $\dfrac{\text{satellite}}{\text{planet}} = \dfrac{\rule{2cm}{0.4pt}}{\text{sun}}$ /moon, comet, earth, star

40. $\dfrac{\text{profit}}{\text{sale}} = \dfrac{\rule{2cm}{0.4pt}}{\text{recreation}}$ /pleasure, sport, activity, strength

* * * * * *

152

5*1*22

PICTURED ANALOGIES

Write in the blank space of each exercise below the letter of the drawing which makes the two ratios similar in their relationships.

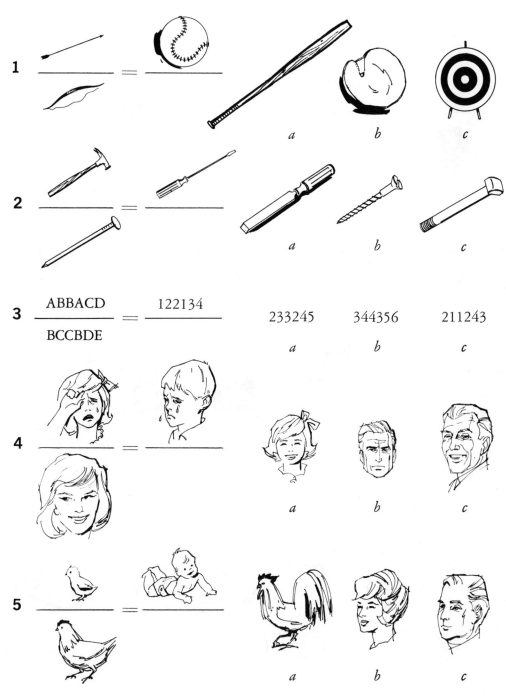

3

ABBACD	122134
BCCBDE	

233245   344356   211243

a   b   c

6

a   b   c

7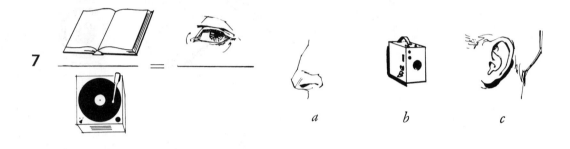

a   b   c

8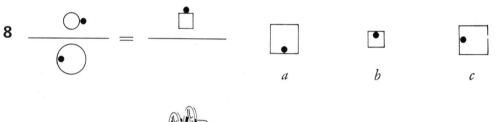

a   b   c

9

a   b   c

10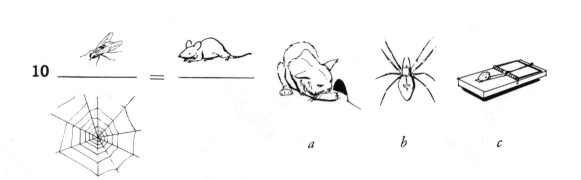

a   b   c

11 _____ = _____   *a*   *b*   *c*

12 _____ = _____   *a*   *b*   *c*

13 _____ = _____   *a*   *b*   *c*

14 _____ = _____   *a*   *b*   *c*

15 _____ = _____   *a*   *b*   *c*

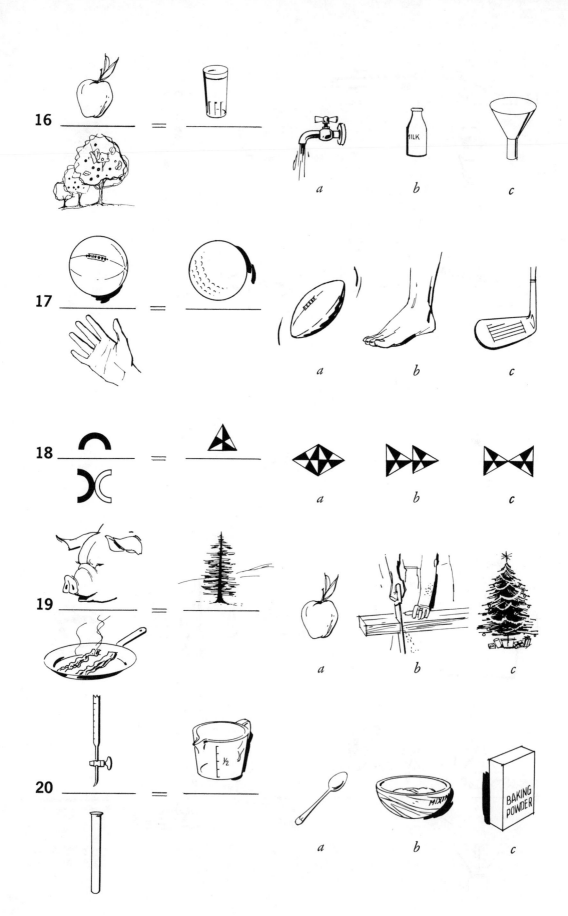

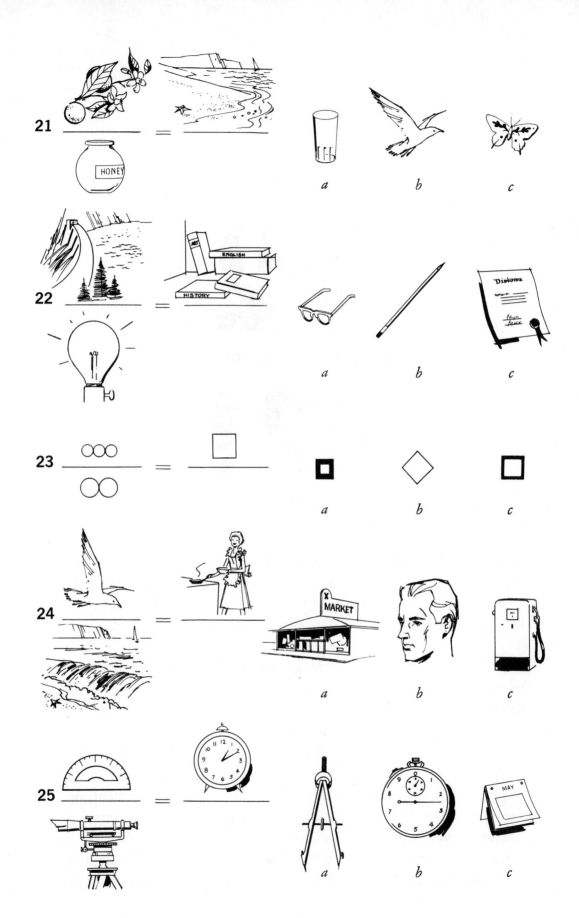

SIMILE AND METAPHOR

TEXT

Although you'll seldom see proportional analogies in the form given in the previous two exercises (except in Miller analogy tests and workbooks such as this), they are a major part of language and, as such, function as the most complex way that words take on new meanings.

We choose to use the term *metaphor* to describe implicit proportional relationships when they occur in speech or writing, but we must remind you that not everyone limits *metaphor* in this way. Some, like Aristotle, include similitudes, and some include explicit expressions of comparison, such as *similes,* as well. Similes differ from metaphors only in the manner of their statement. When we use similes, there is no semantic growth; the words don't take on new meanings. We expressly state a comparison: she is *like* a rose; he was mad *as* a hatter. In a metaphor the metaphorical terms take on new senses, if only temporarily. "Hard work is the key to success" is a metaphor because the relationship it expresses is implicit. It is stated that hard work *is* a key, not that it is *like* a key. The word *key* acquires a new sense. A key is now something other than a device to open a lock. In Shakespeare's *Hamlet* Polonius advises his son,

> This above all, to thine own self be true,
> And it must follow as the night the day
> Thou canst not then be false to any man.

This analogy, which states that truthfulness to others follows truthfulness to oneself just as surely as night follows day, is a simile because the relationship it expresses is explicit. Night is not truthfulness to others nor is day truthfulness to oneself. The words *night* and *day* operate with their old senses. Semantic growth does not take place.

Nearly all our most common, and most useful, words have senses which are metaphorical, or proportionally analogous. The heart of a man differs radically in structure from the heart of a frog, but the two organs perform analogous functions. Consequently the word *heart* serves as a name for both. The heart of a city, the heart of a plant such as celery, and the heart of a disagreement differ from each other as well as from the heart of a man or animal. But all of these things are central or vital elements of some larger entity. This common relationship, in spite of other qualities of dissimilarity, justifies the use of the single word *heart* as the name for each. We may speak of a high mountain, a high price, a high voice, high treason, and a high ambition. Each use of *high* signifies a relationship which is analogous with the relationship of every other use of *high.* A high price is not high in elevation like a high mountain, but both are the upper extremes of their classes. A high ambition is not high in pitch as is a high voice, but both occupy the upper end of some scale. Though *high,* in its metaphorical uses, represents quite different qualities, a unity of meaning is retained because the mind is able to see that each use signifies the upper extent of something (in a very broad and perhaps metaphorical sense of the word *upper*). We may use the word *wing* to mean the wing of an airplane, the wing of a bird, the wing of a building, or the wing of an organization, such as a political party. The verb *cut* may mean to cut an object, such as meat; to cut a path; to cut cards; to cut grease, said of soap or other cleansers; or to cut in the sense of changing direction quickly (as, The halfback cut to the right). We may speak of a dead man, a dead battery, a dead language, a dead tennis ball, a dead issue, or a dead microphone. Our dictionaries contain thousands of words having analogous senses.

Metaphors and their elements inhabit what may be called *universes of discourse,* which are of three sorts: analogical, contextual, and meta. A universe of discourse is a world (or sphere) of things, thoughts, and words. The analogical universe is the universe from which familiar relationships and terminology are borrowed. The contextual universe is the universe to which relationships and terminology are transferred. The metauniverse is a comprehensive universe which includes the other two. It is a genus which contains the others as species. A metaphor is the result when the terminology of one universe of discourse is *transferred* to another. (In fact, *metaphor* is a Greek word meaning "transfer.") In *Hamlet,* Bernardo says to Horatio concerning the ghost which he and Marcellus had previously encountered on their watch,

> Sit down awhile,
> And let us once again assail your ears,
> That are so fortified against our story,
> What we two nights have seen.

The analogical universe, from which the terms *assail* and *fortified* are borrowed, is the universe of war or battle. The contextual universe is the universe of communication. Bernardo and Marcellus wish to *assail* with their words the *fortified* ears (or understanding) of Horatio. By transferring the terms of one world of thought into another, Shakespeare enables us to see a relationship (or analogy) between a mind which is reluctant to believe a report and a structure which is fortified against attack. The metauniverse is the comprehensive world of thought, including both the universe of battle and the universe of communication as species. In any metaphor (or proportional analogy), the analogical universe is the universe from which terminology and relationships are borrowed; it is usually more precise, more concrete. The contextual universe is the universe into which terminology is transferred and similar relationships are observed; it is usually more abstract. For example, in the previous metaphor, the analogical universe concerns battles and describes a relationship between armies and fortified structures, while the contextual universe concerns communication and the more abstract relation of words to understanding. The metauniverse is the universe in which you must think in order to comprehend the similarity between the relationships of the other two universes, and it is the most abstract of all.

Every metaphor involves a similarity between the relationships of two ratios consisting of two things each. In the *Hamlet* metaphor an attacking army is related to a fortified structure, as Bernardo and Marcellus, in the telling of their story, are related to the ears (or understanding) of Horatio. The attacking army and the fortified structure are things in the analogical universe. Bernardo and Marcellus and the ears (or understanding) of Horatio are things in the contextual universe. Every analogy involves two ratios, one in the analogical universe and one in the contextual universe. The similarity between the relationships of these two ratios is observed in the metauniverse.

The relationships between things in the ratios of a metaphor may be expressed by explicit statements. We may say that an army, in the analogical universe, "once again assails a fortified" structure; and that Bernardo and Marcellus, in the contextual universe, "retell the story of the ghost to Horatio in order to convince his reluctant" ears (or understanding). By such statements we signify the relationships between the things of an analogy and thus express its meaning. The relevant relation (or similarity) between the two relationships is expressed by the statement, "once more attempt to overcome the resistance of."

An analogy may also be analyzed in diagrammatic form, as in the example below:

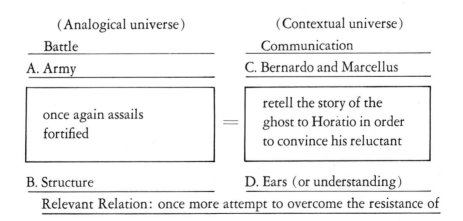

161

The analogical universe is the universe of battle; the contextual universe is the universe of communication. The things and the terminology expressing them and their relations exist within these two universes. The terminology of the relevant relation and the relevant relation itself exist in the comprehensive metauniverse. The thing army and the thing structure in the analogical universe are related to each other *as* are the things Bernardo and Marcellus and the thing ears (or understanding) in the contextual universe. "Once again assails fortified" expresses the relationship between the things in the analogical universe. "Retell the story of the ghost to Horatio in order to convince his reluctant" expresses the relationship between the things in the contextual universe. The similarity between these two relationships is expressed by the genus term (or relevant relation) in the metauniverse, "once more attempt to overcome the resistance of." The relevant relation is the "reason" for the analogy: it is the "meeting point" of the two ratios.

Metaphors are not just pleasing additions to speech or writing. They are instruments of creative thinking. When a known relationship between things in a familiar universe is transferred to a new world of thought, insight (or the discovery of a new relationship) is the result. The old relationship is a species of a hypothetical genus. Insight is the discovery of a new species and the simultaneous crystallization of a genus (or relevant relation) including them both. Metaphorical analysis enables us to see and understand the unfamiliar and gain additional insight into the familiar by controlling language symbols and, thereby, the thoughts they stand for.

EXERCISES

5 * 2 * 2 * 1

COMMON METAPHORS

Following is a list of frequently used expressions. They might be called bywords or clichés, and sometimes they are called dead metaphors because we usually think only of their contextual meanings and rarely recall their analogical meanings. Think of a situation in which each expression might now be said, and name the contextual universe you've placed it in. Then try to name the analogical universe; your dictionary will be a useful reference.

1. Where there's smoke there's fire.
2. He was hoist with his own petard.
3. He's got a hard row to hoe.
4. It's the shank of the evening.
5. He showed his hand.
6. Beware of Greeks bearing gifts.
7. She's either got to fish or cut bait.
8. It's curtains for me.
9. They're fishing in troubled waters.
10. She was the only one to come out of it with clean hands.
11. He died with his boots on.
12. Now for a look behind the scenes.
13. They've surely opened Pandora's box this time.
14. Hold your horses!
15. They were left high and dry.
16. She knows the ropes.

5*2*2

COMMON WORDS USED METAPHORICALLY

The first five metaphors of this section have been partially diagrammed. Fill in the blank spaces with appropriate words or phrases. Analyze each of the remaining metaphors by creating your own diagram on a separate sheet of paper.

1. OLD SENSE: He put on his *coat.*
   NEW SENSE: This barn needs a *coat* of paint.

   (Analogical universe)   (Contextual universe)

   Apparel   Protective coverings

   A. _____   C. Layer of paint

   | keeps cold weather from | = | keeps eroding, or other deteriorating substances, from |

   B. Man   D. _____

   RELEVANT RELATION: keeps harmful agencies from

2. OS: *Fruits* are plant products.
   NS: Poverty and hatred are *fruits* of war.

   (Analogical universe)   (Contextual universe)

   _____   War

   A. Fruits   C. Poverty and hatred

   | | = | are consequences of |

   B. Plants   D. _____

   RR: _____

3. OS: The reservoir has a great *capacity.*
   NS: He has a great *capacity* for knowledge.

   (Analogical universe)   (Contextual universe)

   Physical world   Psychology

   A. _____   C. _____

   | | = | |

   B. Water   D. _____

   RR: _____

164

4. OS: A *magazine* is a storage place, as a warehouse or explosives depot.
   NS: "To how many *magazines* do you subscribe?"

      (Analogical universe)   (Contextual universe)

Structures

A. _____   C. _____

is a storage place for	=	

B. _____   D. _____

RR: is a thing which keeps together in one place

5. OS: A *branch* is a bough.
   NS: Calculus is a *branch* of mathematics.

      (Analogical universe)   (Contextual universe)

A. _____   C. _____

	=	

B. _____   D. _____

RR: is a main division of

6. OS: The mountain climber was killed by an *avalanche*.
   NS: The President's veto brought an *avalanche* of criticism.

7. OS: The drilling went quickly until they hit *bedrock*.
   NS: Few salesmen were able to penetrate the *bedrock* of his thrifty nature.

8. OS: Priests are *benign* people.
   NS: It was a *benign* illness.

9. OS: The cowboy *bridled* his horse.
   NS: One must *bridle* his dreams with common sense.

10. OS: His arm was *broken* in a fall.
    NS: The silence was *broken* by a scream.

11. OS: A *calf* is the offspring of a cow.
    NS: The pirates landed on the *calf*, which was a half mile southeast of the larger island.

12. OS: Many carpenters have *callous* hands.
    NS: Mussolini must have been a *callous* person.

13. OS: There was a natural *channel* between the two lakes.
    NS: Newspapers are a *channel* of communication.

14. OS: They had to portage the canoe around the *chute*.
    NS: The laundry slid down the *chute*.

15. OS: She *coddled* the eggs.
    NS: His mother has *coddled* him all his life.

16. OS: The machine has several *cogs.*

    NS: He is a major *cog* in the company.

17. OS: The ship *collapsed* in the waves.

    NS: His argument *collapsed* when the facts were made known.

18. OS: She *compressed* the cotton into a hard ball.

    NS: He *compressed* the essay into a short paragraph.

19. OS: The horse was *confined* in the corral.

    NS: The debate was *confined* to the subject of religion.

20. OS: A *connection* is a device which joins two or more objects.

    NS: "What is the *connection* between inflation and wage increases?"

21. OS: The Romans *conquered* the Celts.

    NS: He *conquered* his fear.

22. OS: The *core* of the apple was rotten.

    NS: The *core* of his philosophy was a belief in predestination.

23. OS: The baby was asleep in his *cradle.*

    NS: Ancient Greece was the *cradle* of Western philosophy.

24. OS: This pot is *crazy;* it has three cracks on it.

    NS: He was committed to an institution because he was *crazy.*

25. OS: *Cream* is a dairy product.

    NS: The plays of Shakespeare are the *cream* of English drama.

26. OS: The actor missed his *cue.*

    NS: The cloudy sky should have been his *cue* to take a raincoat.

27. OS: The farmer *cultivated* the soil before planting the crop.

    NS: She will never be a writer unless she *cultivates* her mind.

28. OS: She *cut* the cake.

    NS: He *cut* the cards.

29. OS: He ate a *cut* of pie.

    NS: He got a *cut* of the profit.

30. OS: This is a *deep* well.

    NS: He has a *deep* voice.

31. OS: The pirates boarded the *derelict.*

    NS: The Main Street mission was full of *derelicts.*

32. OS: The pilot *deviated* from the course.

    NS: The professor *deviated* from his topic.

33. OS: The doctor *diagnosed* the illness.

    NS: The general *diagnosed* the situation before making his decision.

34. OS: The rabbit *died* from a rattlesnake bite.

    NS: The wind *died* when the rain started to fall.

35. OS: The melting ice *diluted* the lemonade.

    NS: The minister *diluted* his sermon with humorous anecdotes.

36. OS: This wheel is *eccentric*.
    NS: Rich men are sometimes *eccentric*.

37. OS: The sun was *eclipsed* by the moon.
    NS: News of the local election was *eclipsed* by the news that Pearl Harbor had been bombed.

38. OS: The custodian *elevated* the flag.
    NS: His commanding officer *elevated* him to the rank of corporal.

39. OS: She walked to the *end* of the pier.
    NS: Death is the *end* of life.

40. OS: The lights *faded* as the curtain rose for the third act.
    NS: Her smile *faded* when she saw that he was angry.

41. OS: The horse's *flank* was bruised by the spur.
    NS: The enemy's right *flank* began to retreat.

42. OS: He is a *freshman* at Harvard.
    NS: The new African states are entering *freshmen* in the school of nations.

43. OS: He has *gone* to the store.
    NS: "The pain in my leg has *gone*."

44. OS: The headlights *illuminated* the street ahead.
    NS: The sermon *illuminated* for her the meaning of *Genesis*.

45. OS: The material was *imbued* with green dye.
    NS: He was *imbued* with the desire to become a doctor.

46. OS: The porter *labeled* the luggage before putting it on the train.
    NS: They *labeled* him a Communist.

47. OS: An arm is a *member* of the body.
    NS: He is a *member* of the YMCA.

48. OS: His face was *obscure* in the darkness.
    NS: An *obscure* politician was nominated for the presidency.

49. OS: The medulla is a *part* of the brain.
    NS: What *part* of your vacation did you like best?

50. OS: He *quenched* the fire with water.
    NS: He *quenched* his thirst with a glass of lemonade.

51. OS: The moon is a *satellite* of the earth.
    NS: Hungary is a Russian *satellite*.

52. OS: Mrs. Timmons is a *widow*.
    NS: He forgot to deal the *widow*.

53. OS: She *wove* a mat of straw.
    NS: He *wove* his minor troubles into a story of hardship.

54. OS: The sun is at its *zenith*.
    NS: The emperor was at the *zenith* of his power.

5*2*3

ANALOGICAL QUOTATIONS

The first three analogies of this section have been partially diagrammed. Fill in the blank spaces with appropriate words or phrases. Analyze each of the remaining analogies by creating your own diagram on a separate sheet of paper.

Before you analyze each analogy you should determine in your own mind whether it is a metaphor or a simile. In a simile the languages of two different universes are before your eyes and the relationship between the proportional elements is "spelled out" for you. But in a metaphor you are confronted with the language of *one* universe (the analogical) in a world where it "doesn't belong." *You* must provide, in the contextual universe, the appropriate language and the things which the language denotes. Because of this need to "fill in" missing elements metaphors are characteristically more difficult to comprehend than similes.

1. [In speaking of the effects of education Plato says that a philosopher is] like a plant which, having proper nurture, must necessarily grow and mature into all virtue, but, if sown and planted in an alien soil, becomes the most noxious of all weeds, unless he be preserved by some divine power.

Plato, *The Republic,* in *Great Books of the Western World,* VII, p. 377.

(Analogical universe)		(Contextual universe)
_____		Education _____
A. _____		C. Philosopher
will either grow and mature into a good plant or into a noxious weed depending on whether it is given proper nurture in a good or sown and planted in an alien	=	
B. _____		D. Education

RR: will either develop into a good specimen or a bad one

depending on whether it is given proper care in a

good or made to endure the effects of a bad

2. [In the first chapter of *Moby-Dick* Ishmael, the narrator, states,] I cannot tell why it was exactly that those stage managers, the Fates, put me down for this shabby part of a whaling voyage...

Melville, op. cit., p. 5.

(Analogical universe)
_____

A. Stage managers
_____

[ ] =

B. _____

RR: _____

(Contextual universe)
Life
_____

C. _____

[ ]

D. _____

3. When sorrows come, they come not single spies,
But in battalions...

Shakespeare, Hamlet, IV, v, 78-79.

(Analogical universe)
Warfare
_____

A. _____

[ ] =

B. _____

RR: _____
_____

(Contextual universe)
_____

C. Sorrows
_____

[ ]

D. _____

4. THE Lord *is* my shepherd...

Psalms 23:1.

5. An institution is the lengthened shadow of one man; as, Monachism, of the Hermit Antony; the Reformation, of Luther; Quakerism, of Fox; Methodism, of Wesley; Abolition, of Clarkson.

Ralph Waldo Emerson, "Self-Reliance."

6. [In refuting the idea that the earth is the center of the universe Copernicus asks,] ... why not admit that the appearance of daily revolution belongs to the heavens but the reality belongs to the Earth? And things are as when Aeneas said in Virgil: "We sail out of the harbor, and the land and the cities move away." As a matter of fact, when a ship floats on over a tranquil sea, all the things outside seem to the voyagers to be moving in a movement which is the image of their own, and they think on the contrary that they themselves and all the things with them are at rest. So it can

easily happen in the case of the movement of the Earth that the whole world should be believed to be moving in a circle.

Nicolaus Copernicus, On the Revolutions of the Heavenly Spheres,
in Great Books of the Western World, XVI, p. 519.

7. KNOW you not, that you are the temple of God, and that the Spirit of God dwelleth in you?

I Corinthians (Douay Version) 3:16.

8. [William James states that without memory] our consciousness would be like a glow-worm spark, illuminating the point it immediately covered, but leaving all beyond in total darkness.

James, op. cit., p. 396.

9. [The ghost of his father reminds Hamlet to avenge his murder, by saying,] Do not forget. This visitation
Is but to whet thy almost blunted purpose.

Shakespeare, Hamlet, III, iv, 111-12.

10. ...sense-perception testifies that exactly as it is with the six planets around the sun, so too is the case with the four satellites of Jupiter: in such fashion that the farther any satellite can digress from Jupiter, the slowlier does it make its return around the body of Jupiter.

Johannes Kepler, Epitome of Copernican Astronomy, in
Great Books of the Western World, XVI, p. 918.

11. Some books are to be tasted, others to be swallowed and some few to be chewed and digested...

Francis Bacon, "Of Studies."

12. ENTER ye in at the narrow gate: for wide is the gate and broad is the way that leadeth to destruction, and many there are who go in thereat.

How narrow is the gate and strait is the way that leadeth to life: and few there are that find it!

Matthew (Douay Version) 7:13-14.

13. [When Laertes reminds his sister to remember the advice he has given her, she replies,]

'Tis in my memory locked,
And you yourself shall keep the key of it.

Shakespeare, Hamlet, I, iii, 85-86.

14. [In Moby-Dick Ishmael imagines Queequeg saying to himself, after rescuing a bumpkin from the sea,] It's a mutual, joint-stock world, in all meridians. We cannibals must help these Christians.

Melville, op. cit., p. 61.

15. A moment's halt — a momentary taste
Of BEING from the Well amid the Waste —
    And lo! the phantom Caravan has reached
The NOTHING it set out from... Oh, make haste!

Edward Fitzgerald, Rubáiyát of Omar Khayyám, XLVIII.

16. [In evaluating Hamlet's moody behavior following the murder of his father, Claudius, the murderer, says,]

> There's something in his soul
> O'er which his melancholy sits on brood,
> And I do doubt the hatch and the disclose
> Will be some danger...

Shakespeare, Hamlet, III, i, 164-67.

17. Society is a wave. The wave moves onward, but the water of which it is composed does not. The same particle does not rise from the valley to the ridge. Its unity is only phenomenal. The persons who make up a nation to-day, next year die, and their experience dies with them. Emerson, *op. cit.*

18. [Father Mapple, in *Moby-Dick,* describes as follows Jonah's torment in his flight from God:]

Screwed at its axis against the side, a swinging lamp slightly oscillates in Jonah's room; and the ship, heeling over towards the wharf with the weight of the last bales received, the lamp, flame and all, though in slight motion, still maintains a permanent obliquity with reference to the room; though, in truth, infallibly straight itself, it but made obvious the false, lying levels among which it hung. The lamp alarms and frightens Jonah; as lying in his berth his tormented eyes roll around the place, and this thus far successful fugitive finds no refuge for his restless glance. But that contradiction in the lamp more and more appals him. The floor, the ceiling, and the side, are all awry. "Oh! so my conscience hangs in me!" he groans, "straight upward, so it burns; but the chambers of my soul are all in crookedness!"

Melville, op. cit., pp. 43-44.

19. It is customary to regard the course of history as a great river, with its source in some small rivulet of the distant past, taking its rise on the plains of Asia, and flowing slowly down through the ages, gathering water from new tributaries on the way, until finally in our own days it broadens majestically over the whole world.

John Herman Randall, Jr., The Making of the Modern Mind,
Boston, Houghton Mifflin Company (1949), p. 9.

20. No man is an island, entire of itself; every man is a piece of the continent, a part of the main; if a clod be washed away by the sea, Europe is the less, as well as if a promontory were, as well as if a manor of thy friend's or of thine own were. Any man's death diminishes me, because I am involved in mankind.

John Donne, "Meditation 17," in Devotions Upon Emergent Occasions.

21. Oh Thou, who didst with pitfall and with gin
    Beset the road I was to wander in,
       Thou wilt not with predestined evil round
    Enmesh, and then impute my fall to sin!

Fitzgerald, *op. cit.,* LXXX.

22. There's a divinity that shapes our ends,
    Rough-hew them how we will —

Shakespeare, *Hamlet,* V, ii, 10-11.

23. [The passage below contains two metaphors, the "stoneless grave" metaphor and the "lee shore" metaphor.]

Some chapters back, one Bulkington was spoken of, a tall, new-landed mariner, encountered in New Bedford at the inn.

When on that shivering winter's night, the Pequod thrust her vindictive bows into the cold malicious waves, who should I see standing at her helm but Bulkington! I looked with sympathetic awe and fearfulness upon the man, who in mid-winter just landed from a four years' dangerous voyage, could so unrestingly push off again for still another tempestuous term. The land seemed scorching to his feet. Wonderfullest things are ever the un-mentionable; deep memories yield no epitaphs; this six-inch chapter is the stoneless grave of Bulkington. Let me only say that it fared with him as with the storm-tossed ship, that miserably drives along the leeward land. The port would fain give succor; the port is pitiful; in the port is safety, comfort, hearthstone, supper, warm blankets, friends, all that's kind to our mortalities. But in that gale, the port, the land, is that ship's direst jeopardy; she must fly all hospitality; one touch of land, though it but graze the keel, would make her shudder through and through. With all her might she crowds all sail off shore; in so doing, fights 'gainst the very winds that fain would blow her homeward; seeks all the lashed sea's landlessness again; for refuge's sake forlornly rushing into peril; her only friend her bitterest foe!

Know ye, now, Bulkington? Glimpses do ye seem to see of that mortally intolerable truth; that all deep, earnest thinking is but the intrepid effort of the soul to keep the open independence of her sea; while the wildest winds of heaven and earth conspire to cast her on the treacherous, slavish shore?

But as in landlessness alone resides the highest truth, shoreless, indefinite as God — so, better is it to perish in that howling infinite, than be inglori-ously dashed upon the lee, even if that were safety! For worm-like, then, oh! who would craven crawl to land! Terrors of the terrible! is all this agony so vain? Take heart, take heart, O Bulkington! Bear thee grimly, demigod! Up from the spray of thy ocean-perishing — straight up, leaps thy apotheosis!

Melville, *op. cit.,* pp. 104-05.

5*22*4

CREATION OF FUNCTIONAL ANALOGIES

Create and analyze an analogy as suggested in each exercise below.

1. Write a metaphor using flower growing as your analogical universe and child rearing as your contextual universe.

2. Design a grocery store display of cans or boxes analogous to an Egyptian pyramid.

3. Write a metaphor using warfare as your analogical universe and courtship as your contextual universe.

4. Design a garden wall analogous to a sheet of corrugated metal. What advantages might such a wall have?

5. Write a simile using farming as your analogical universe and teaching or education as your contextual universe.

6. Apply the principle of musical harmony to a social situation.

7. Write a metaphor using fishing as your analogical universe and salesmanship as your contextual universe.

8. Transfer the concept of the "mind's eye" to the universes of hearing, tasting, and the other sensory modalities.

9. Write a metaphor using anatomy as your analogical universe and law enforcement as your contextual universe.

10. Transfer the "team spirit" idea to some social, economic, or political project.

11. Write a metaphor using space travel as your analogical universe and vocations as your contextual universe.

12. How might a salesman improve his selling technique, reasoning by analogy from the principle of the thermometer?

13. Write a simile using mountain climbing as your analogical universe and human relationships as your contextual universe.

14. Suggest a practical method of birth control, reasoning by analogy from the principle of the governor.

15. Write a metaphor using medicine as your analogical universe and crime and punishment as your contextual universe.

16. What suggestions might you make to improve a system of automobile traffic regulation, reasoning by analogy from the human circulatory system?

17. Write a metaphor using weaving as your analogical universe and conversation as your contextual universe.

18. Think of several areas in which the principle of the thermostat might be applied.

19. Write a metaphor using sculpture as your analogical universe and God's creation of the world as your contextual universe.

20. Invent a new water sport analogous to baseball.

21. Write a metaphor using dancing as your analogical universe and astronomy as your contextual universe.

22. Alter an unsuccessful phase of your life by analogy with a successful phase.

23. Write a simile using gold mining as your analogical universe and scientific research as your contextual universe.

24. What are the consequences of comparing the soul to a tenant in a burning house, to a brief pain in the leg, or to the water poured into a glass from a pitcher? To what other things might the soul be compared?

25. Write a metaphor using bowling as your analogical universe and human emotions as your contextual universe.

26. Paint or draw a picture which is analogous to a piece of music which you enjoy. Or compose a piece of music which is analogous to a work of art which you admire.

27. Write a simile using baking as your analogical universe and reading as your contextual universe.

28. Apply the principle of progressive resistance (in weight lifting) to educational philosophy.

29. Write a metaphor using weather as your analogical universe and dreams as your contextual universe.

30. Think of several possible areas in which the principle of the polarization of light might be applied.

31. Write a metaphor using sailing as your analogical universe and decision making as your contextual universe.

32. Try to find a practical use, in any field, for the principle of the moebius strip.
33. Write a simile using geography or geology as your analogical universe and human motivation as your contextual universe.

34. Plan a rearrangement of some organization, such as a business, educational institution, or club, reasoning by analogy from the three-branch form of the United States government.

35. Write a metaphor using lighting (lamps, candles, etc.) as your analogical universe and love as your contextual universe.

36. Develop a new method, design a new structure, or reach a new insight by the use of analogy.

37. Write a poem, essay, or story containing one or more significant metaphors or similes.

38. Make a working classification of all the possible uses for analogies.

DEFINITION

SECTION 6

SORTS OF DEFINITION

TEXT

There are seven basic kinds of definition which may be used separately or in combination:

> SYNONYM
> ANTONYM
> EXEMPLIFICATION
> COMPARISON
> CLASSIFICATION
> STRUCTURE ANALYSIS
> OPERATION ANALYSIS

SYNONYM

A synonym is a word which has a sense that is the same as a sense of another word. *Automobile* is a synonym for *car* if *car* means "four-wheeled motor vehicle," but not if *car* means "elevator cage" or "railroad car." A synonym is usually an ambiguous symbol which when used in a particular context has a sense which is the same as the sense of another ambiguous symbol when used in another particular context.

ANTONYM

An antonym is a word which has a sense that is the opposite of a sense of another word. Because there are numerous senses of the word *opposite,* a given word may have numerous antonyms. *Red* may be an antonym for *green* if we are concerned with the position of colors on the color wheel, but in the playing card universe it may be an antonym for *black.* The word *opposite* may call into play sensory, affective, and logical qualities. Logical opposition may involve classification, structure, and operation considerations. In certain contexts *red* and *green* are antonyms, having senses which are opposite in the sensory quality of color; *lovely* and *ugly* have senses which are opposite in the emotional quality of beauty; senses of *large* and *small* may be opposite in the logical quality of size. Antonyms may signify opposing ends of scales of sensation such as sight, hearing, taste, and smell; of emotion such as fear, anger, love, and awe; or of logical relation such as size, shape, number, space, and time. Words such as *well* and *sick* may have opposite senses which involve combinations of sensory, affective, and logical qualities. Analytic considerations may be involved when senses are opposite in logical qualities. *Ceiling* and *floor* are antonyms when we consider the structure of a room. *Birth* and *death* signify opposite stages in the operation of life. And classification is a means by which certain judgments of opposition are made. *Hot* and *cold* stand for opposite ends of a graduated scale which may be considered a *class* of temperature experiences. *Man* and *animal* stand for opposite categories signified by the two branches of a dichotomous classification.

EXEMPLIFICATION

Definition by exemplification is definition by example. An example is a specimen. A particular cat is a specimen of some named class such as cats or animals. The word *animal* may be exemplified by pointing to a particular cat, a particular horse, and other particular creatures or by saying, "This cat, horse, squirrel, zebra, or lizard is an animal."

There are two ways of "pointing" in the act of exemplification. We may point literally or we may "point" with words. But in either case we indicate certain examples (specimens) of some genus. The word *dog* may be exemplified by pointing to Rover or by saying, "Rover is a dog." If the world is at peace we may define *war* by pointing with words to the Korean War or to World War II.

We may also exemplify words by pointing literally or with words to photographs, drawings, or other representations of things. The word *mountain* may be exemplified by pointing to a photograph of the Matterhorn or by saying, "That photograph has a mountain in it." Representations, so used, are not really examples but representations of examples. Definition by exemplification is the process of indicating directly or indirectly particular specimens of genus terms.

<h2 style="text-align:center">COMPARISON</h2>

Comparison is like exemplification except that each example offered is accompanied by a statement of how it differs from the referent of the word being defined. The word *ocean* may be defined by saying, "An ocean is like a lake but larger." The word *animal* may be defined by saying, "An animal is like a tree except that it moves by itself and is not connected to the ground." The word *king* may be defined by saying, "A king is like George Washington except that he is not elected by the people." In the process of comparison a genus may be compared with another genus, a genus may be compared with a species of another genus, or a genus may be compared with a specimen of another genus. In the examples above the genus ocean is compared with the genus lake, the genus animal is compared with the species tree, and the genus king is compared with the specimen George Washington.

While exemplification is a process of indicating a referent of a word, comparison is a process of indicating a thing which is similar to a referent but different in specified ways.

<h2 style="text-align:center">CLASSIFICATION</h2>

There are three sorts of analytic definition: definition by classification, by structure analysis, and by operation analysis.

Definition by classification is a deliberate process involving a species term, a genus term, and a differentia. A species term is a word to be defined; a genus term is a word with a sense which includes the sense of the word to be defined; and a differentia is a statement which indicates the quality which differentiates the sense of the species term from all other species included by the meaning of the genus term. In the definition, "A woman is an adult, female human being," *woman* is a species term because it signifies a kind of human being; *human being* is a genus term because it signifies a class including women as a species; and *adult, female* is a differentia because it distinguishes the sense "woman" from all other species of the sense "human being." In the definition, "A tree is a plant with roots, a trunk, and branches," *tree* is a species term because it signifies a kind of plant; *plant* is a genus term because it signifies a class including trees as a species; and *with roots, a trunk, and branches* is a differentia because it distinguishes trees from all other species of plants.

In defining by classification the following rules should be kept in mind. The genus term, in order to *be* a genus term, must have a more general meaning than the species term to be defined, and the differentia must distinguish the species in question from all other species of the genus. *Human being* is a genus term for *woman* because it has a meaning which includes the meaning of *woman*. *Adult, female* is an adequate differentia because it indicates how women are different from all other species of human beings. But neither *adult* nor *female* by itself would be an adequate differentia. An adult human being or a female human being may be called a man or girl, respectively, as well as a woman.

STRUCTURE ANALYSIS

A second type of analytic definition is definition by structure analysis. Names of parts, wholes, and joints may be defined by this method. The name of a part may be defined by naming the whole and indicating how it is connected to the parts which adjoin it. The name of a structural whole may be defined by naming the principal parts and by indicating how they fit together. The name of a joint may be defined by indicating how it divides two or more parts of a whole.

In the definition, "An arm is a part connected to the hand and shoulder of the human body," *arm* is the name of a part to be defined; *human body* is the name of a whole; and *connected to the hand and shoulder* is a statement which both "isolates" the arm from the other parts of the body and indicates its connection with adjacent parts.

In the definition, "A pencil is a structure composed of a rod-shaped casing usually of wood, metal, or plastic enclosing throughout its length a rod usually of graphite extending at one end, when ready for use, to a point slightly beyond the casing," *pencil* is the name of a whole to be defined; *rod-shaped casing* is the name of a principal part; *rod* is the name of another principal part; and the words *enclosing . . . extending . . . slightly beyond the casing* compose a statement of how the two main parts are connected to each other.

In the definition, "A shoreline is the edge of a body of water dividing it from land," *shoreline* is the name of a joint to be defined, and *body of water* and *land* are names of parts of the whole (land *and* water) which are divided by the shoreline.

By structure analysis the name of a part may be defined by referring to its whole, by distinguishing the part from the other parts of the whole, and by indicating the connections the part has with adjacent parts; the name of a whole may be defined by referring to the main parts of the whole and by indicating how these parts fit together; or the name of a joint may be defined by indicating the whole and the parts of the whole which are divided by the joint.

OPERATION ANALYSIS

Definition by operation analysis is appropriate whenever words to be defined are the names of operations or elements of operations. An operation is a structure changing for a purpose in time and space. The operation of such a changing structure may be divided into stages and/or phases. A changing structure is composed of changing parts. A changing part (or a phase) has a function in an operation. An operation has a purpose. Names of the following eight operational concepts may be defined by operation analysis:

OPERATION

STAGE

STRUCTURE (changing)

PART (changing)

PHASE

JUNCTURE

FUNCTION

PURPOSE

The name of any one of these concepts may be defined by referring to any of the remaining concepts. The name of an operation may be defined by referring to such elements as the stages of the operation, its moving structure, the articulation of the moving parts of the structure, the function of the moving parts in the operation of the moving structure, or the purpose of the operation. The name of a stage may be defined by referring to such elements as the operation of which it is a "part" or the relationship of the stage to preceding and/or succeeding stages. The name of a phase may be defined by referring to such elements as the operation of which it is a "part," the stages of the phase, the "parallel" stages of other phases, or the function of the phase. The name of a function may be defined by referring to such elements as an appropriate part, structure, operation, or purpose. *Webster's New World Dictionary* gives this operational definition of *rocket:*

> ... a projectile consisting of a cylinder filled with a combustible
> substance which when ignited produces gases that escape through
> a vent in the rear and drive their container forward by the prin-
> ciple of reaction ...

Rocket, the word defined, is the name of a changing, when operational, structure. The operation, though unnamed, is implied to be the ignition and flight of a rocket. Three stages are mentioned: the ignition of a combustible substance, the production of gases, and the escape of these gases causing movement. Three functional parts (or phases) are mentioned: a cylinder, a combustible substance inside, and a vent in the rear. The function of the phase of the cylinder is implied to be that of containing the combustible substance and providing a projectile. The function of the phase of the combustible substance is implied to be that of producing gases and thereby providing propulsion; the function of the phase of the vent is apparently that of guiding the escape of the gases. The purpose of the changing structure or of the operation might, according to various circumstances, be flight, transportation, or destruction.

SUMMARY

Words may be defined by verbal substitution or by direct reference to the things they signify. Synonyms and antonyms are verbal substitutes. If we define *car* by referring to *automobile,* we are merely replacing one word with another. If we use *hot* to define *cold* we are defining a word by exchanging it for another word with an opposite sense. In either case we are substituting one symbol for another on the chance that an appropriate association may exist between the substituted symbol and a sense which will point out the sense of the symbol to be defined.

Unlike definition by synonym or antonym, definition by exemplification, comparison, classification, structure analysis, or operation analysis involves a direct reference to things. If we define *car* by pointing to a car, we are not trading one word for another; we are making a direct reference to a specimen of the class represented by *car,* cutting out the verbal middleman. If we say what a car is a sort of and how it differs from other sorts of that sort; if we say what the parts of a car are and how they fit together; or if we say how a car works, we are likewise defining the word *car* by making direct reference to things, though we may use words in the process.

Definitions which refer to things have to do with analysis in either a rudimentary or deliberate way. Exemplification and comparison involve the genus-species relation, but not deliberately or systematically. We probably are not aware that we are classifying when we define *animal* by pointing to a dog or when we define *bush* by saying, "It's like a tree except smaller."

But by the analytic methods of classification, structure analysis, and operation analysis words are defined on purpose by a process involving explicit statements of genus, species, whole, part, operation, stage, and other appropriate analytic concepts. Because of their complexity analytic definitions may often be difficult to distinguish as to the sort of analysis involved. In general a definition is classificational if the mind is thinking in terms of genus and species; a definition is structural if the mind is thinking in terms of whole and part; and a definition is operational if the mind is thinking in terms of operation, stage, and related concepts such as function and purpose. The definition, "A neck is a connection supporting the head on the shoulders," is a classificational one if we are thinking of a neck as a species of the genus connection, in which case *supporting the head on the shoulders* is a differentia. But the definition is a structural one if we are concerned with the neck as a part of the body as a *whole,* in which case *supporting the head on the shoulders* serves to name adjacent parts and their spatial relationships to the neck. But if we are thinking of support as a *function* of the neck, the definition is an operational one, support, in this context, involving operational forces of gravity, momentum, and muscular tension. The sort of analysis involved in a definition is determined by the analytic operation going on in the mind of the definer. Often an intelligent guess is the best answer to the question of whether a definer is thinking in terms of classification, structure analysis, or operation analysis. All three sorts of analysis may be contained in a complex definition. But in this section we are concerned primarily with simple, basic, or "pure" definitions.

6*1*2

EXERCISES

6*1*2*1

CLASSIFICATION OF DEFINITIONS

In the following exercise write the sorting factors on the appropriate lines and put the letters of the specimens in the appropriate pigeonholes.

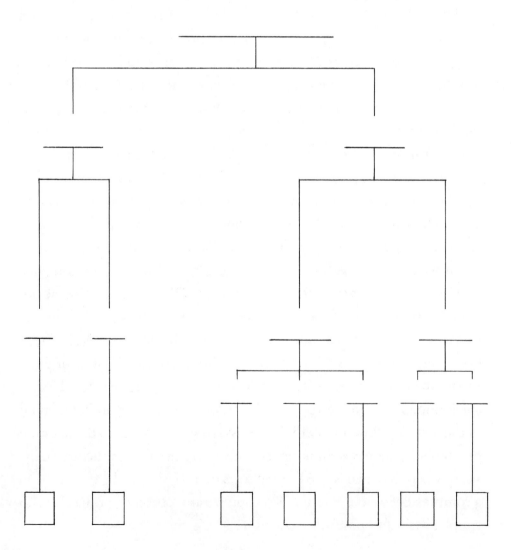

1. Exemplification
2. Operation analysis
3. Rudimentary analysis
4. Synonym
5. Direct reference to things
6. Structure analysis

7. Definitions of words
8. Antonym
9. Verbal substitution
10. Comparison
11. Classification
12. Deliberate analysis

SPECIMENS:

a. He rode a black *mare.* (Opposite of *stallion*)

b. The *man* crossed the street. (A man is an adult, male human being.)

c. He likes bacon better than *fat back.* (Fat back is the top part of a hog. It extends from the ham to the head section and borders on its lower surface the loin and shoulder.)

d. She had a *chance* to go to Europe. *(Opportunity)*

e. He picked a *flower.* ( )

f. He has two *sisters.* (A sister is like a brother except that she's a girl.)

g. After Jane sang the first verse we all joined in for the *chorus.* (A chorus is the part of a musical performance in which several voices in unison follow a solo.)

h. Use your *fork,* not your knife. (A fork consists of a handle and two or more tines at one end.)

i. The precinct *numbered* 175 people. *(Totaled)*

j. She wants to be a *writer.* (John Steinbeck)

k. Venus is a *planet.* (A planet is like a star except that it shines by reflected solar light.)

l. One should learn to *speak* clearly. (To speak is to communicate orally.)

m. Some *roots* are edible. (A root is the part of a growing plant which grows into the soil and supplies nourishment to the rest of the plant.)

n. The air was *freezing* outside. (Opposite of *warm*)

o. *Christianity* is a major religion. (Christianity is similar to Hinduism except for the belief in one god.)

p. The *cellar* was flooded during the last rain. (A cellar is an underground room often used for storage purposes.)

q. The lost boy was *starving. (Going hungry)*

r. The *keystone* was cut by hammer and chisel. (A keystone is the central wedge-shaped part of an arch which by its position exerts an outward and downward pressure on the adjacent stones, holding them in place.)

s. It was an *elevating* experience. (Opposite of *degrading*)

t. "What does *picnic* mean?" ("That was a picnic we had last week when we packed a lunch and went to the country.")

u. She drew a *square* in the sand. (A square is composed of four equal straight lines connected at their ends in a closed figure of four right angles.)

6*1*2*2

Define on a separate sheet of paper the italicized word of each exercise.

SYNONYM

With the aid of your dictionary find a synonym for the italicized word in each sentence below.

1. He threw a *rock* into the pond.
2. The earthquake caused the house to *rock*.
3. The *stone* was an emerald.
4. He removed the *seed* from the peach.
5. I *see* what you mean.
6. She is a *relation* by marriage.
7. She started to *press* the clothes.
8. *Place* it on the table.
9. He was third in line but lost his *place*.
10. *Admit* no one but the doctor.

ANTONYM

With the aid of your dictionary define by antonym each italicized word below.

11. The dog has a *loud* bark.
12. She wore a *lovely* dress.
13. Water is a *liquid*.
14. The car was a *bright* red.
15. *Many* people attended the reception.
16. The barn was made of *flimsy* materials.
17. The people *frustrated* the dictator's scheme.
18. Jane was *frustrated* after being turned down for the job.
19. The sun is not really on fire, except in a *loose* sense.
20. The lawyer advised his *principal* to accept the offer.

EXEMPLIFICATION

Exemplify each of the italicized terms below by drawing pictures of or by "pointing" with words to specific things.

21. There is a *painting* in the hallway.
22. A *dime* is worth ten pennies.
23. Have you ever seen a *movie star?*
24. What is that *book* you're reading?
25. *Vowels* and consonants are letters.
26. There are many *skyscrapers* in New York.
27. What sort of *car* do you have?
28. Most *countries* belong to the United Nations.
29. *Christmas* comes once a year.
30. Economic stability will be maintained by a proper balance between production and *consumption*.

Define each italicized term below by comparison.

31. The *porthole* was clouded with fog.

32. The *yams* were delicious.

33. He lost his *pen.*

34. The prisoner tried to escape from his *cell.*

35. *Fruit* is plentiful in California.

36. She went to *college.*

37. *Laws* are not always enforced.

38. He was full of *envy.*

39. The woman *ran* for the train.

40. The *traffic* on the freeway was heavy.

CLASSIFICATION

In each exercise below define the italicized word by classification. Then circle the species term of your definition, put a single line under the genus term, and put a double line under the differentia.

41. A *man* and a woman boarded the bus.

42. The earth is a *planet.*

43. *Lunch* was served at 12:30.

44. He glanced at his *watch.*

45. A potato is a sort of *vegetable.*

46. The *lake* was covered with ice.

47. A bear is a *mammal.*

48. The dog began to *whine.*

49. The *blanket* was blue.

50. The *theory* of evolution is well-established.

STRUCTURE ANALYSIS

Define each italicized word below by structure analysis. In your definition put a circle around the name of the whole, put a single line under the name(s) of the part(s), and put a double line under the words which indicate connections among relevant parts.

51. Monkeys and squirrels have *tails.*

52. One *leaf* was torn from the book.

53. *Ladders* are useful devices.

54. Dinner was on the *table.*

55. His *sleeve* was dirty.

56. The *eye* is a spherical organ.

57. The *heart* is a vital organ.

58. The *door* was open.

59. She mended the tear with *thread.*

60. The *forest* was dark.

In each exercise below define the italicized word by operation analysis. Then indicate which of the following operational elements names the word as defined:

operation
stage
structure
part
phase
juncture
function
purpose

Then indicate to which operational elements the defining words refer. An example has been worked for you.

EXAMPLE

The rifle has a long *barrel.*

Definition	Word defined	Name of ...	Defining words	Names of ...
A barrel is a hollow cylindrical part of a gun which guides a projectile as it is ejected by an explosive charge.	*barrel*	part	*gun* *guides* *projectile* *ejected* *explosive charge*	structure phase part phase part

61. Rowboats do not have *sails.*

62. She enjoyed cutting the material from the pattern but disliked the actual *sewing.*

63. The *sole* of his shoe was worn.

64. The *clock* was slow.

65. The sound was good but faulty *projection* due to a dirty lens caused the image to be blurred.

66. While the men in the boiler room were shoveling coal, the pilot was *steering* the steamship down the Mississippi.

67. They played ten *hands* of poker.

68. He hoped to *profit* from the investment.

69. Gandhi's *fast* lasted a month.

70. A man's *skeleton* is different from a woman's.

6*2

DEFINITION OF WORDS USED IN SINGLE SENSES

6*2*1

TEXT

In practice, adequate definition of a word in a single sense may consist of any or all of the seven basic sorts of definition. If we wish to define the word *car* thoroughly, we may begin with the synonym "automobile"; proceed to the classification definition, "a four-wheeled vehicle which normally travels by road, street, or highway"; continue with a structure analysis definition, describing the parts of a car and how they fit together; go on to an operation analysis definition, telling how a car works; and perhaps end with a definition by exemplification, such as a picture or a diagram of a car.

6*2*2

In each exercise below define on a separate sheet of paper the italicized word by the methods indicated.

1. He took his *girl* to a dance.
   SYNONYM
   COMPARISON
   CLASSIFICATION

2. America's *servicemen* are well-trained.
   SYNONYM
   ANTONYM
   EXEMPLIFICATION

3. Jimmy got a *velocipede* for Christmas.
   SYNONYM
   COMPARISON
   STRUCTURE ANALYSIS
   OPERATION ANALYSIS

4. *Hunting* is a popular sport.
   ANTONYM
   COMPARISON
   CLASSIFICATION
   OPERATION ANALYSIS

5. A polar *day* is different from an equatorial day.
   EXEMPLIFICATION
   CLASSIFICATION
   OPERATION ANALYSIS

6. A *quality* is a component of a thing.
   SYNONYM
   ANTONYM
   EXEMPLIFICATION
   CLASSIFICATION

7. A *buttress* adds strength to a building.
   COMPARISON
   STRUCTURE ANALYSIS
   OPERATION ANALYSIS

8. *Death* is seldom very painful.
   SYNONYM
   ANTONYM
   CLASSIFICATION
   OPERATION ANALYSIS

9. His writing was almost completely free of *tropes.*
   SYNONYM
   EXEMPLIFICATION
   CLASSIFICATION

10. The Standard Oil Co. is a dynamic *organization.*
    SYNONYM
    EXEMPLIFICATION
    COMPARISON
    OPERATION ANALYSIS

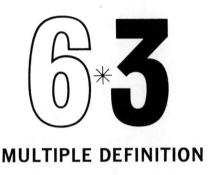

MULTIPLE DEFINITION

TEXT

A more complex definitive act than the indication of a single sense of a word is multiple definition, the indication of several senses of a word. By multiple definition we not only gain an awareness of the variety of senses a word may have but we also enable ourselves to "define" (set the limits to) a particular meaning which may be of immediate interest to us. A multiple definition of the word *man* might include definitions such as the following:

> Human being, whether male or female, child or adult
> An adult male
> An adult, male servant
> To provide with men who serve a function
> A brave or self-reliant man

Such a multiple definition might help us to choose the sense most appropriate to a sentence such as, "Man requires food and sleep." Knowing that *man* has a sense applying to male adults only might cause us to take care to select a definition which includes women and children as well as "men." It is often relevant for us to know what a word does *not* mean, as well as what it means, in a given context.

EXERCISES

In each exercise below give at least five senses of the italicized word by any or a combination of any of the seven forms of definition. Then choose a definition appropriate to the word as used in the sentence.

1. Will atomic war destroy the *world?*

2. He had a splinter *beneath* his fingernail.

3. Is it a *dress* affair?

4. Her *ears* were sunburned.

5. I'll see you *in* church Sunday.

6. In America all men have *equal* opportunity.

7. Does the *soul* survive death?

8. It is a *paradox* to say that a man's father was childless.

9. He may have committed a crime but he did nothing *wrong*.

10. The café was *empty* except for the waitress.

11. How is the law of gravitation affected by the *theory* of relativity?

12. Someone has to control even a *free* press.

13. The ambassador's bad manners were *glossed* over by the newspapers.

14. If he was in Florida at the time, *then* he couldn't have stolen the jewels.

15. *True* vegetarians do not consume animal products of any sort, not even milk or cheese.

PROBLEM-SOLVING

TEXT

Solving problems by manipulating symbols—by using language—is something we do every day. Most problems are simple and we can solve them without much effort, without need for rigorous analysis. We keep track of our checking accounts by adding and subtracting numbers; we make decisions concerning food and clothing purchases based on the size of our checking accounts, our likes and dislikes, our needs, and so forth. Very often we need never articulate the problem or the decision.

But some problems are complex. They involve the consideration of multiple relationships among a large body of data. We cannot solve these problems intuitively because we cannot keep all the facts and their ramifications in mind easily. Reorganization of a business, creation of a curriculum, election of a party candidate, and eradication of a disease are all examples of complex problems that have complex solutions—that involve many kinds of facts with many kinds of relationships.

Problem solving is an operation with three general stages:

PLANNING

EXECUTION

EVALUATION

A problem-solver plans the solution of a problem, executes the plan, and evaluates the results. These stages have a parallel in the legislative, executive, and judicial branches of our government. The Congress passes laws (plans governmental functions); the President determines a policy for administering (or executing) the laws of the land; and the Supreme Court rules upon the constitutionality of laws passed by the legislature and actions performed by the President (evaluates the acts of the other two branches). Actually, though each branch is *primarily* concerned with planning, execution, or evaluation, all three problem-solving stages function in the deliberations of each. The President, for example, *plans* a method of administering the laws passed by Congress and *evaluates* the results of his administration. In the *Book of Genesis* God's acts of creation may be divided into planning, execution, and evaluation stages. "And God said, Let us make man in our image..." (planning). "So God created man in his *own* image..." (execution). "And God saw every thing that he had made, and, behold, *it was* very good," (evaluation). Deciding what to do, doing it, and examining what you have done are the three fundamental stages of solving a problem. Below is a list of words which may act as synonyms for the terms *planning, execution,* and *evaluation.*

PLANNING	EXECUTION	EVALUATION
Deciding	Administration	Judging
Designing	Doing	Appraising
Projecting	Performing	Conclusion
Scheming	Effecting	Reviewing
Plotting	Carrying out	Discerning
Preparation	Production	Estimating
Legislating	Enforcing	Weighing

If a problem-solver *plans* to plan, execute, and evaluate, the operation of his analysis may be summarized as follows:

    1. Planning
        1. Planning
        2. Execution
        3. Evaluation
    2. Execution
    3. Evaluation

Planning (at position 1) has the sense of "planning, together with planning to execute and planning to evaluate." *Planning* (1-1) has the sense of "planning — exclusive of considerations of the stages of execution and evaluation." *Execution* (2) has the sense of "actual execution." *Execution* (1-2) has the sense of "planned execution." *Evaluation* (3) has the sense of "actual evaluation." *Evaluation* (1-3) has the sense of "planned evaluation." A problem-solver may plan by planning what to do, planning how to do what he has decided to do, and by planning how to evaluate what he will have done. After he has thus planned he may actually execute his plan and evaluate the results.

Following is an outline of a relatively complete method of problem-solving. The outline should be considered a check list rather than a sequence of precisely consecutive stages. Every problem has nuances which require a unique procedure, different from all others. But the solutions of all problems have elements which are similar, though the order and scope of the elements may differ in specific cases.

1. PLANNING
    1. Planning
        1. Statement of general problem and its elements
            1. Statement of general problem
            2. Statement of phases and/or stages of problem
        2. Definition of terms of problem and terms of elements of problem
            1. Multiple definition
                1. Multiple definition of terms of statement of general problem
                2. Multiple definition of terms of statement of phases and/or stages of problem
            2. Working definition
                1. Working definition or restatement of general problem
                2. Working definition or restatement of phases and/or stages of problem
        3. Hypothesis
            1. Working hypothesis for general problem
            2. Working hypotheses for phases and/or stages of problem
        4. Analysis
            1. Classification
                1. Working classification
                    1. Working classification(s)
                    2. Collection and pigeonholing of specimens and revision of working classification(s)
                2. Classification of collected specimens
            2. Structure analysis
                1. Analysis(es) of planned structure(s)
                2. Analysis(es) of existing structure(s)

3. Operation analysis

    1. Analysis(es) of planned operation(s)

    2. Analysis(es) of past or existing operation(s)

5. Induction and deduction

    1. Inductions and deductions after each phase and/or stage of problem

    2. Inductions and deductions relevant to the general problem

2. Execution (planned)

3. Evaluation (planned)

2. EXECUTION (actual)

    1. Execution of the existing plan

    2. Replanning where necessary and execution of elements of revised plan

3. EVALUATION (actual)

    1. Evaluation after execution of each phase and/or stage of plan

    2. Evaluation after execution of entire plan

Of the stages listed in the elaborate outline above, seven are usually essential to the solution of any complex problem and will provide the focus for the remainder of our work here:

TENTATIVE STATEMENT OF PROBLEM

MULTIPLE DEFINITION OF KEY TERMS

WORKING DEFINITION, OR RESTATEMENT, OF PROBLEM

WORKING HYPOTHESIS

WORKING CLASSIFICATION

COLLECTING AND PIGEONHOLING SPECIMENS

RELEVANT INDUCTIONS AND DEDUCTIONS

Remember that any particular problem-solving process may involve additional stages as well as unmentioned substages. And the order of stages may vary considerably from the "ideal" sequence presented above. Digression and reevaluation, for example, nearly always occur in the solution of problems of considerable difficulty. While the list is incomplete for practical purposes, it is comprehensive in the sense that it includes considerations which are basic to the solution of most problems, whatever additional factors may command our attention in specific cases.

TENTATIVE STATEMENT

A tentative statement is simply a beginning statement, usually in question form, of your problem. It is the source for all the remaining steps. Sometimes a rewording of it will lead to new directions or insights if the problem-solving operation breaks down. Examples of tentative statements are: Are men or women more intelligent? Which candidate will the Republicans nominate for president at the next convention? Who is the most significant character in *Middlemarch?* What are Captain Ahab's attitudes toward religion (in *Moby Dick*)?

MULTIPLE DEFINITION

By examining all the possible meanings for each of the terms in the tentative statement, the maximum number of choices of both problem and methods for solution can be discovered. Begin by listing all the possibly relevant senses from an unabridged dictionary. Consider definitions of *all* terms: *key* terms are not always immediately apparent. Here are six definitions of *religion* from *Webster's Third International Dictionary* that are relevant to the tentative statement, What are Captain Ahab's attitudes toward religion?

1. The personal commitment to and serving of God or a god with worshipful devotion, conduct in accord with divine commands especially as found in accepted sacred writings or declared by authoritative teachers, a way of life recognized as incumbent on true believers, and typically the relating of oneself to an organized body of believers.
2. One of the systems of faith and worship; a religious faith.
3. The body of institutional expressions of sacred beliefs, observances, and social practices found within a given cultural context as in "The religion of this primitive people."
4. The profession or practice of religious beliefs: religious observances.
5. A personal awareness or conviction of the existence of a supreme being or of supernatural powers or influences controlling one's own, humanity's or all nature's destiny.
6. The access of such an awareness or conviction accompanied by or arousing reverence, gratitude, humility, the will to obey and serve; religious experience or insight.

These six definitions of this one term alone lead to a number of possibilities. We could consider Captain Ahab's attitudes toward one or more of a number of things: particular religious practices or beliefs, a particular established faith, a primitive religion, certain primitive religious practices, God, Fate, and so on.

This is the most crucial stage. An adequate restatement identifies precisely *what* you want to find out and *how* you're going to find it out. From your list of multiple definitions, choose the definition for each word that most closely fits your purpose. Make each of these definitions more specific— expand them, qualify them, set specific boundaries. Definition by classification, structure analysis, operation analysis, or a combination will usually be the most useful. Dictionary definitions are good starting places, but they must be refined to fit the particular problem at hand; they must identify the relevant data for that specific case.

An *in*adequate restatement for Which character was most significant in *Middlemarch?* would be Which character in the book *Middlemarch* by George Eliot had the largest degree of importance or meaning? We still have no guide for determining what is important or meaningful, or significant. The potential data are as elusive as ever. An *in*adequate restatement for Are men or women more intelligent? would be Are adult males or adult females more likely to have a greater mental capacity? Again, we have no more idea of the qualities of "mental capacity" than we did of "intelligent."

An adequate restatement of What are Captain Ahab's attitudes toward religion? based on definition 3 above might be: What are Captain Ahab's attitudes toward certain religious practices of Queequeg's? Captain Ahab and Queequeg are characters in Herman Melville's *Moby Dick* and are represented by the printed lines which describe their physical attributes, their mental and emotional states, and their actions. This problem concerns the lines that explicitly describe Ahab's approval or disapproval of Queequeg's observance of Ramadan, worship of the idol Yojo, and burial-rite practices. The lines may be dialogue attributed to Captain Ahab or dialogue by other characters about Ahab's approval or disapproval of these religious practices of Queequeg's. An adequate restatement based on definition 5 above (note that this choice of meaning for *religion* leads to the need for a definition of *God*) might be: What are Captain Ahab's attitudes toward God? (Or, Does Captain Ahab believe in God?) Captain Ahab is a character in Herman Melville's *Moby Dick* represented by the printed lines which describe his physical attributes, his mental and emotional states, and his actions. This problem concerns the lines that explicitly describe his belief or disbelief in God as the creator, sustainer, judge, righteous sovereign, and/or redeemer of the universe. The lines may be dialogue attributed to Captain Ahab, narrative descriptions of his thoughts, or dialogue by other characters about Ahab's belief in God.

WORKING HYPOTHESIS

Some problems, even after adequate definition, still do not show clearly what sort of data will provide a solution because several kinds of data could provide valid answers. These are "puzzle" problems that need a working hypothesis—a statement that names the specific data considered useful for analysis. Deciding whether men or women are more intelligent is a problem of this kind. No matter what qualities we assign *intelligent,* we are still left with many choices of valid measurements of intelligence—various IQ tests, SAT scores, grade-point averages, and so forth. A working hypothesis states which of these we believe will yield a valid answer and therefore identifies which statistics to collect.

An example of a literary puzzle problem would be, What was Herman Melville's opinion of women as expressed in *Moby Dick?* No matter how we define *opinion* or *women,* these definitions don't direct us to the kinds of data that reveal Melville's own attitude because *Moby Dick* is a novel, not a biography, and the author's views are implicit. He might express his opinion through Ishmael, the narrator character, or through all the male characters, or through references to women in the Bible, or through references to the female of any species, and so forth. A working hypothesis is needed to show which of these we've chosen to yield our answer. A restatement and working hypothesis of this problem might be: What was Herman Melville's opinion of women as expressed in his novel *Moby Dick?* His ideas about which character traits and roles should be common to women are those he assigns the female characters (such as loyalty, devotion, and patience; housewife, mother, sweetheart). The lines collected may be narrative descriptions or dialogue explicitly naming a trait or role of a woman character. The extended Example II, Will the Democratic majority in the Senate kill the Pork Bill? on pages 209-213, shows a working hypothesis to a nonliterary puzzle problem.

A working classification is an explicit statement in diagram form of the data you plan to collect. Your restatement should yield your classification sorting factors; if it is adequate it includes all the qualities you will need to begin gathering and sorting data. One branch of your classification may have more levels than another. All qualities are not relevant to all branches. Therefore, the horizontal sorting factor at a given level may differ from branch to branch. For example, in the following working classification for the Ahab problem, the branch According to Other Characters would need to be divided into vertical sorting factors naming specific characters, but it would not be divided into In Narration and In Dialogue, because our restatement specifies only dialogue in relation to the other characters. Notice, too, that each level of the classification relates to a qualification in the restatement. Level (1) deals with "lines attributed to Ahab . . . or dialogue by other characters about Ahab"; level (2) deals with "lines [that] may be dialogue attributed to Ahab [or] narrative descriptions of his thoughts"; level (3) deals with "lines explicitly describing his belief or disbelief in God"; and level (4) deals with the characteristics of God—"creator, sustainer, judge, righteous sovereign, and/or redeemer."

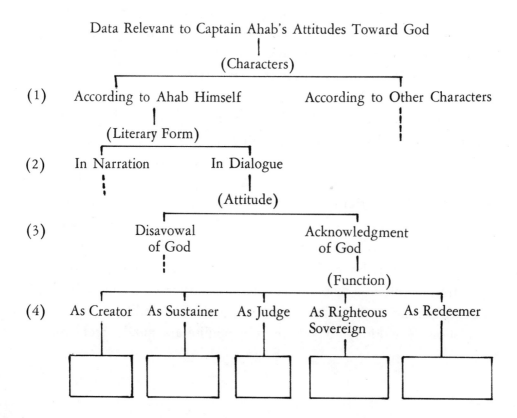

Data Relevant to Captain Ahab's Attitudes Toward God

(Characters)

(1) According to Ahab Himself   According to Other Characters

(Literary Form)

(2) In Narration   In Dialogue

(Attitude)

(3)   Disavowal   Acknowledgment
           of God   of God

(Function)

(4) As Creator   As Sustainer   As Judge   As Righteous   As Redeemer
                                            Sovereign

Data may be collected by recording information on cards or sheets of paper (although cards are less cumbersome for actual sorting). Each card equals one specimen. Here are examples for the Ahab problem:

```
┌─────────────────────────────────────────────────┐
│ Ahab—dialogue                                     │
│ God as righteous sovereign              card  1   │
├───────────────────────────────────────────────────┤
│   "There is one God that is Lord over the          │
│   earth, and one Captain that is lord over         │
│   the Pequod."                                     │
│                                        page  471   │
└─────────────────────────────────────────────────┘
```

```
┌─────────────────────────────────────────────────┐
│ Ahab—dialogue                                     │
│ God as creator                          card  2   │
├───────────────────────────────────────────────────┤
│   (Ahab describes the physical position of        │
│   man's eyes.)                                     │
│                                                    │
│   "Level by nature to this earth's horizon are     │
│   the glances of man's eyes; not shot from the     │
│   crown of his head, as if God had meant him to    │
│   gaze on his firmament."                          │
│                                        page  494   │
└─────────────────────────────────────────────────┘
```

```
┌─────────────────────────────────────────────────┐
│ Ahab—dialogue                                     │
│ God as redeemer                         card  3   │
├───────────────────────────────────────────────────┤
│   (Ahab addressing Pip)                            │
│                                                    │
│   True art thou, lad, as the circumference to      │
│   its centre. So: God for ever bless thee;         │
│   and if it come to that,—God for ever save        │
│   thee, let what will befall."                     │
│                                        page  525   │
└─────────────────────────────────────────────────┘
```

```
┌─────────────────────────────────────────────┐
│  Ahab—dialogue                                │
│  God as sustainer                    card 4   │
│ ┌───────────────────────────────────────────┐│
│ │ "But if the great sun move not of itself; but││
│ │ is as an errand-boy in heaven; nor one single││
│ │ star can revolve, but by some invisible power;││
│ │ how then can this one small heart beat; this ││
│ │ one small brain think thoughts; unless God  ││
│ │ does that beating, does that thinking, does ││
│ │ that living, and not I."                    ││
│ │                              page 536       ││
│ └───────────────────────────────────────────┘│
└─────────────────────────────────────────────┘
```

Use the following checklist to guide your collecting and sorting:

1. Gather all the data relevant to your problem. Omitting data skews the results.

2. If your specimens don't fit your working classification, ask yourself if your data are relevant and if your working classification is complete.

3. Each specimen goes in one pigeonhole only. If a specimen could go in more than one pigeonhole, check to see that your sorting factors are mutually exclusive and that the data card doesn't actually contain more than one specimen.

4. Empty pigeonholes may be significant. They can show which expected or possible traits, beliefs, or conditions are absent—whether Ahab indeed believes in God, whether Melville attributes only passive traits to women, and so forth.

The result of gathering all relevant data according to your purpose and sorting it adequately according to the qualities relevant to your purpose is a final classification.

INDUCTIONS AND DEDUCTIONS

Inductions and deductions are the two species of the genus inference which is a species of logic or reason. It is as essential to be able to tell them apart as it is to recognize the type of analysis going on in one's head in a given moment of the problem-solving process. We may say that inductions and deductions are applications of the rules or laws of reason.

Inductions are basic to our understanding of the various "universes" in which we live. In classification, inductive law is a species that has the characteristics of its genus, so we may say "all these pigeons" only after we have examined them all. In structure analysis we may not say "this pigeon here" until we have determined that as a pigeon it *is* all there. In operation analysis we may say, "This is Columbine, my prize pigeon, hatched in the spring of 1976, banded in late summer, and placed in this cage for today's show," only after examining the bird, the band, and the ticket on the cage. All such statements are inductions. *Deductions* are logical applications of the opposite sort. They proceed from the genus to the species, from the general to the specific. Tumbler pigeons somersault in flight. That pigeon just did a somersault. It must be a tumbler.

In problem-solving we seek conclusions, which are either inductions or deductions or combinations of both.

These seven stages of problem-solving are exemplified in the following two problems. Example II is a puzzle problem; Example I is not.

EXAMPLE I

Ten weightlifters were gathered at a gymnasium for a contest. Weightlifter number 1 pressed (lifted over his head from the shoulders) a 145-pound barbell. Number 2 lifted 275 pounds six inches off the ground. Number 3 pressed 125 pounds. Number 4 pressed 260 pounds. Number 5 pressed 140 pounds with one hand, arguing later that he could have lifted 280 pounds with two hands. Number 6 pressed 270 pounds. Number 7 pressed 190 pounds. Number 8 pressed a 75-pound barbell five times in a row, arguing later that he had lifted a total of 375 pounds. Number 9, who was five feet tall, lifted a 280-pound barbell over his head from the top of a rack six feet high. Number 10 pressed 265 pounds. Number 8's brother arrived at the gymnasium after the competition was over and pressed 295 pounds. Who won the contest?

This problem is not a puzzle and may be solved simply by manipulating and evaluating data after clear definition has taken place.

STAGE ONE: TENTATIVE STATEMENT OF PROBLEM

Assuming that winning the contest is dependent upon success in lifting weight, the problem may tentatively be stated as follows: "Which of the contestants lifted the most weight?"

The following definitions were selected from *Webster's New World Dictionary*.

which

1. What one (or ones) of the number of persons, things, or events mentioned or implied?: as, *which* of the men answered? *which* do you want?

2. A thing or fact that: as, you are late — *which* reminds me, where were you yesterday?

3. Whatever; no matter what: as, try *which* method you please, you cannot succeed

  ✳ Others

contestant

  A person who contests or competes in a contest

contest

1. To try to disprove or invalidate (something), as by argument or legal action; dispute: as, he will *contest* his father's will

2. To fight for (ground, a military position, etc.); struggle to win or keep

3. To contend; struggle (*with* or *against*)

4. Strife; struggle; conflict; fight

5. Verbal strife; controversy; dispute

6. Any race, game, debate, etc. in which there is a struggle to be the winner

lift

1. To bring up to a higher position; raise

2. To pick up and set: as, to *lift* a baby down from its high chair

3. To hold up; support high in the air

4. To change (a person's face) by means of a surgical operation...

5. To exert strength in raising or trying to raise something

6. To rise and vanish; be dispelled: as, the gloom *lifted*

7. The amount lifted at one time

8. Elevation of spirits or mood

9. A ride in the direction in which one is going

10. In *aeronautics,* the upward pull resulting from the force of the air against an airfoil passing through it

  ✳ Others

most

1. Greatest in amount, quantity, or degree: used as the superlative of *much*

2. Greatest in number: used as the superlative of *many*

3. In the greatest number of instances: as, *most* fame is fleeting

  ✳ Others

weight

1. Heaviness as a quality of things; attraction of a material body by gravitational pull toward... the earth: in physics, distinguished from *mass*

2. Quantity or amount of heaviness; how much a thing weighs: as, the *weight* of an egg

3. Any unit of heaviness or mass

4. A piece of metal, wood, etc. of a specific standard heaviness, used on a balance or scale in weighing

5. Any block or mass of material used for its heaviness

6. One used to hold light things down: as, a paper *weight*

7. One used to drive a mechanism: as, the *weights* in a clock

8. One used to maintain balance: as, *weights* placed on an automobile wheel

9. One of a particular heaviness, lifted as an athletic exercise

10. Importance or consequence: as, a matter of great *weight*

11. Any of the several classifications into which boxers and wrestlers are placed according to how much they weigh

12. To add weight to; make heavy or heavier

13. To burden; load down; oppress

14. In *statistics,* to give a weight, or value, to (an item in a frequency list)

✳ Others

STAGE THREE: WORKING DEFINITION OR RESTATEMENT OF PROBLEM

Let us define *which* to mean "what one," not "what ones." If we decide that a contestant is "a person who contests or competes in…any race, game, debate, etc. in which there is a struggle to be the winner," the dictionary has been only partially helpful in our effort to define *contestant*. What does it mean to contest or to compete? The brother of number 8 lifted a barbell but did he compete with the others? Upon careful consideration we may decide that mutual consent to compare performances must precede an act in order for it to be thought of as a competitive one. *Contestant,* as used in the statement of our problem, may then be defined as the name of anyone who has previously agreed to compare his athletic performance with that of others at a given time and place. Several of the contestants lifted barbells over their heads from a shoulder position. All of these, but one, used both hands. One contestant lifted a barbell off the top of a rack which extended twelve inches higher than his head. If we let *lift* mean "to bring up to a higher position; raise," then all of the contestants lifted weight. But let us assign to *lift* the more restrictive sense of "to raise an object over one's head from the shoulders," making it a synonym for *press.* (It is instructive to note that neither this definition of *lift* nor the equivalent definition of *press* appears in the dictionary.) In this sense the definition of *lift* remains insufficiently precise. There are one-handed as well as two-handed lifts.

So let us define *lift* even more precisely to mean "to raise an object over the head from the shoulders with two hands."

Lift, so defined, refers to a single act of raising an object with both hands over the head from the shoulders. But if we were to define *lift* more broadly so that it could also refer to several acts of raising an object over the head from the shoulders, and if we were to define *weight* as the "quantity or amount of heaviness," then we would conclude that number 8 lifted 375 pounds. But let us define *weight* as "any block or mass of material...of a particular heaviness, lifted as an athletic exercise." This definition, together with our original definition of *lift,* causes us to conclude that number 8 lifted a weight of 75 pounds five times, that he did *not* lift 375 pounds. Finally let us define *most* to mean "heaviest," not "largest in size" or "greatest in number."

Using our working definitions we may restate our problem as follows: "Which one of those who had previously agreed to compare performances raised over his head from the shoulders with two hands in a single lift the heaviest barbell?"

STAGE FOUR: WORKING HYPOTHESIS

Since our problem is not a puzzle a working hypothesis is unnecessary. The solution is clearly in sight and all that is needed to reach it is the collection, organization, and evaluation of appropriate data.

STAGE FIVE: WORKING CLASSIFICATION

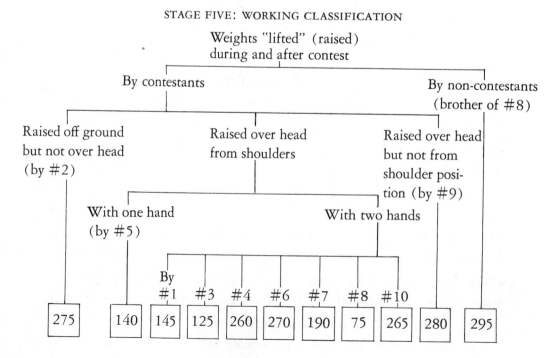

The working classification above does not include the data in the pigeon-holes. The working classification of a problem should be started before data are collected and should grow and otherwise change as information is gathered. The actual collection and pigeonholing of data, however, belong to a later stage.

STAGE SIX: COLLECTION AND PIGEONHOLING OF SPECIMENS

The data, or specimens, have already been collected and have been pigeonholed in the preceding diagram.

STAGE SEVEN: RELEVANT INDUCTIONS AND DEDUCTIONS

The classification diagram enables us to induce, in accordance with our restatement of the problem, that number 6 lifted the most weight.

If we had defined *lift* generally to mean simply "raise," then number 9 would have lifted the most weight. If we had defined *lift* to mean "raise from the shoulders over the head *one or a number of times*" and *weight* to mean "quantity of heaviness," then number 8 would have lifted the most weight, 375 pounds. If we had changed our restatement of the problem so that *contestant* referred to number 8's brother as well as the others, then *he* would have been the contestant who lifted the most weight.

The solution of any problem depends upon the definitions of the terms in which it is stated. A problem "becomes" what it is stated and defined to be. Inductions and deductions are always implications of definitions.

EXAMPLE II

The date is September 12, 1964. According to a Gallup poll the electorate throughout the country are strongly in favor of the Pork Bill, which is up before the Senate. The Democratic administration, however, is desirous of defeating the bill. A majority of the senators are Democrats. Will the Senate pass or defeat the Pork Bill?*

STAGE ONE: TENTATIVE STATEMENT OF PROBLEM

"Will the Democratic majority in the Senate kill the Pork Bill?"

---

*It should be understood that this problem is purely hypothetical and is not intended to bear any relationship to actual political circumstances.

The senses below have been taken from *Webster's New World Dictionary.*

democratic

    1. Of, belonging to, or upholding democracy or a democracy

    2. Considering and treating others as one's equals; not snobbish

    3. [D-], Of, belonging to, or characteristic of the Democratic Party

    * Others

majority

    1. The greater part or larger number; more than half of a total: opposed to *minority*

    2. The excess of the larger number of votes cast for one candidate, bill, etc. over all the rest of the votes: if candidate A gets 100 votes, candidate B, 200, and candidate C, 350, C has a majority of 50: cf. *plurality*

    3. The group, party, or faction with the larger number of votes

    * Others

senate

    1. Literally, a council of elders

    2. The supreme council of the ancient Roman state, originally only of patricians but later including the plebeians

    3. A lawmaking assembly; state council

    4. [S-], A legislative group, generally the smaller, and called the *upper,* of the two houses forming certain national and State legislatures: in the United States Senate there are two senators from each State, regardless of its size

kill

    1. To cause the death of; put to death; slay

    2. To destroy; put an end to; ruin

    3. To prevent the passage of (legislation); defeat or veto

    * Others

STAGE THREE: WORKING DEFINITION OR RESTATEMENT OF PROBLEM

"Will the members of the Democratic Party in the upper house of the United States Congress, who control over half of the votes in that body, prevent the passage of the Pork Bill?"

STAGE FOUR: WORKING HYPOTHESIS

This problem is a puzzle problem, offering two or more avenues of solution. A working hypothesis will allow us to travel down one of these avenues toward a solution which may or may not be true. If we wish to travel down two or more avenues, two or more working hypotheses must be formulated. Without a working hypothesis further progress in a problem of this sort is impossible. Only in a problem which is not a puzzle may a solution be reached by a single route without a working hypothesis to point the way.

How will the Senate vote on the Pork Bill? Our conclusion will be little more than a wild guess unless we follow the plotted course of a working hypothesis. A working hypothesis will enable us to proceed in a given direction by indicating what data to collect in order to reach a valid, though not necessarily true, conclusion. If we could poll the members our problem would not be a puzzle. But lacking time, funds, or opportunity we must resort to the use of a working hypothesis.

Suppose we reason as follows. The Republican senators will follow the electorate in order to embarrass the administration; the secure Democrats will support the administration against the electorate; but the Democrats soon to come up for re-election will bolt in order to please the voting public. Our reasoning leads us to the following working hypothesis: "The fate of the bill depends upon the number of Democrats up for re-election."

Now we know what data to collect. We are after any fact which indicates that a given Democratic senator is or is not about to run for re-election.

STAGE FIVE: WORKING CLASSIFICATION

Suppose we know that fifty-six of the one hundred senators are Democrats. Our job is to find out how many of the fifty-six are up for re-election. The working classification diagram which follows will aid us in our collection of data and will provide a means of organizing the data as they are accumulated. As increasing information creates the need for further differentiation, our classification diagram will sprout additional branches.

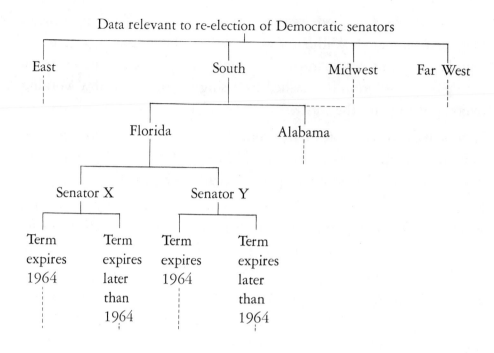

Data relevant to re-election of Democratic senators

East | South | Midwest | Far West

Florida | Alabama

Senator X | Senator Y

Term expires 1964 | Term expires later than 1964 | Term expires 1964 | Term expires later than 1964

Data may conveniently be collected by recording information on cards or on sheets of paper. Here are some samples:

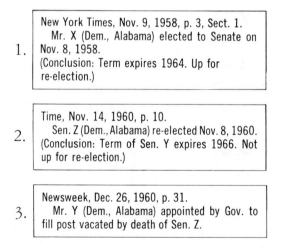

1.
New York Times, Nov. 9, 1958, p. 3, Sect. 1.
Mr. X (Dem., Alabama) elected to Senate on Nov. 8, 1958.
(Conclusion: Term expires 1964. Up for re-election.)

2.
Time, Nov. 14, 1960, p. 10.
Sen. Z (Dem., Alabama) re-elected Nov. 8, 1960.
(Conclusion: Term of Sen. Y expires 1966. Not up for re-election.)

3.
Newsweek, Dec. 26, 1960, p. 31.
Mr. Y (Dem., Alabama) appointed by Gov. to fill post vacated by death of Sen. Z.

Card one would be classified under *Senator X, term expires 1964.* Cards two and three would be classified under *Senator Y, term expires later than 1964.*

Suppose that, when classified, our data indicate that the terms of twenty-four Democratic senators expire in 1964 and that the terms of thirty-two expire later than 1964. Will the Democrats kill the Pork Bill? The data of our classification, together with other pertinent data, are summarized below.

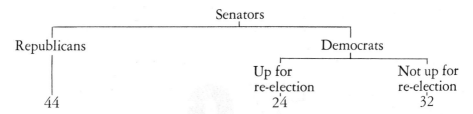

According to our working hypothesis the Republicans and the Democrats up for re-election will vote together in favor of the Pork Bill. The bill will pass sixty-eight to thirty-two.

Our conclusion is "no," the Democratic majority in the Senate will not kill the Pork Bill.

Our conclusion might have been otherwise had we chosen another working hypothesis. Our hypothesis might have been, "The senators will vote on this bill as they have voted on similar bills in the past." Data relevant to this hypothesis would be entirely different from data relevant to our previous hypothesis and when classified might lead to the opposite conclusion. If our hypothesis had been that the senators would vote strictly according to party lines, then our conclusion would have been that the bill would be defeated fifty-six to forty-four.

EXERCISES

7·2·1

TEXT-RELATED EXERCISES

Perform on a separate sheet of paper the operations indicated in each exercise below.

1. State a problem in each of the following areas: politics, athletics, personal affairs, religion, finances, and health. You need not define terms.

2. Give multiple definitions of the terms of each problem statement below. Where possible add your own definitions to those listed in the dictionary. Restate the definitions you take from the dictionary.

    A. Are men more intelligent than women?

    B. Does the end always justify the means?

    C. What is the basic purpose of a liberal education?

3. Choose working definitions for the terms of each problem statement above. Then restate each problem, making use of these definitions. While in the act of restatement you may find it desirable to add new senses to your lists of multiple definitions.

4. Name two working hypotheses for the problem suggested by each question or statement which follows. Remember that a working hypothesis is a statement which indicates a procedure for gathering information when more than one procedure is possible.

A. A man complains of chest congestion to his doctor.

B. How might a farmer predict the rainfall for the coming month?

C. In light of the failure of the League of Nations, why has the United Nations continued to exist?

D. A citizens' committee wants to find a way to combat narcotics addiction in America.

E. Who will be the next president of the United States?

F. An astronomer wishes to determine whether there is any form of life on the moon.

G. How might a person go about finding information to explain Hitler's rise to power?

H. The officials of a college are faced with the problem of determining a wise admissions policy.

I. How might a scholar or scientist determine the age of a vase found in an archaeological excavation?

J. How might a scientist determine the velocity of sound?

5. Make the working classification suggested by each question below.

A. What sorts of building materials are there, if your purpose is to build a house? Your classification should involve at least eight vertical sorting factors.

B. What sorts of provisions are there, if your purpose is to go on a mountain-climbing expedition? Your classification should involve at least twelve vertical sorting factors.

C. What sorts of specimens, or data, are there, if your purpose is to discover the causes of World War II? Your classification should involve at least sixteen vertical sorting factors.

6. Collect fifty words at random from your dictionary and pigeonhole them under the appropriate sorting factors of the working classification diagram below. As you collect them you will probably need to add sorting factors to the branches under *two, three,* and *four or more.*

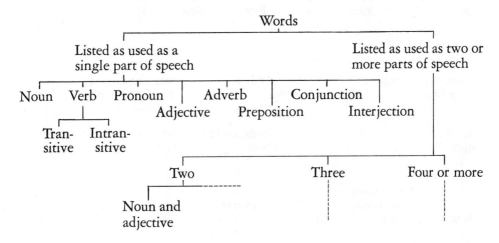

7. Make five inductions and five deductions by referring to the classification diagram which follows.

EXAMPLES:

A. Except for Thomas Jefferson none of the presidents who were also vice-president were elected to office more than once. (Induction)

B. Theodore Roosevelt, who was vice-president before becoming president, was elected to office only once. (This is a deduction from the previous induction. Deduction is a process of reaching conclusions without direct examination of specimens, or data.)

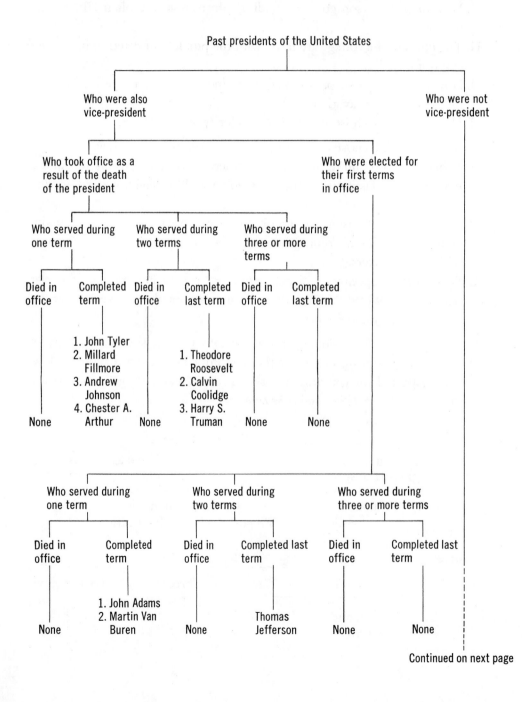

Continued on next page

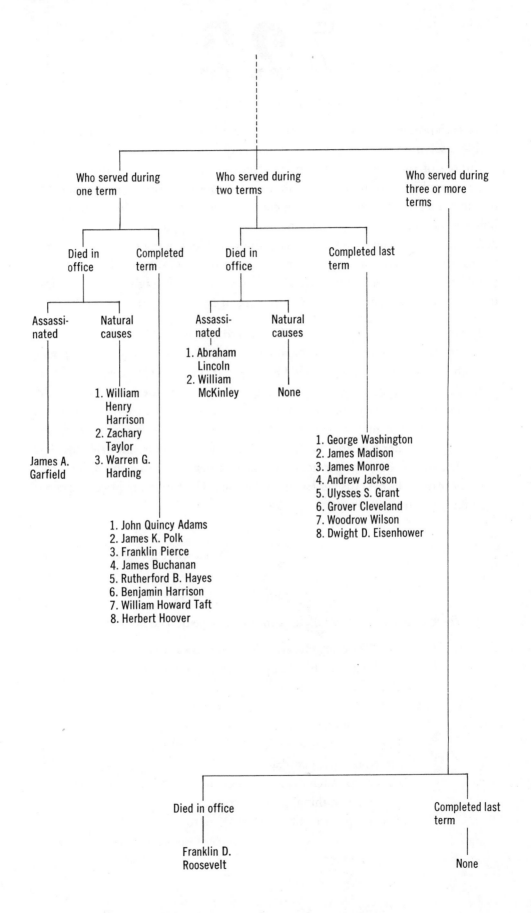

Who served during one term

Died in office

Assassinated

James A. Garfield

Natural causes

1. William Henry Harrison
2. Zachary Taylor
3. Warren G. Harding

Completed term

1. John Quincy Adams
2. James K. Polk
3. Franklin Pierce
4. James Buchanan
5. Rutherford B. Hayes
6. Benjamin Harrison
7. William Howard Taft
8. Herbert Hoover

Who served during two terms

Died in office

Assassinated

1. Abraham Lincoln
2. William McKinley

Natural causes

None

Completed last term

1. George Washington
2. James Madison
3. James Monroe
4. Andrew Jackson
5. Ulysses S. Grant
6. Grover Cleveland
7. Woodrow Wilson
8. Dwight D. Eisenhower

Who served during three or more terms

Died in office

Franklin D. Roosevelt

Completed last term

None

7*2*2

Solve each problem in this section by making explicit use of the seven stages of problem-solving. State the problem in terms of your own choice; give multiple definitions of each term; restate the problem using working definitions chosen from the multiple definitions; formulate one or more working hypotheses, if the problem is a puzzle; make a working classification diagram; collect and pigeon-hole relevant data, or specimens; and finally, make appropriate inductions and deductions. Your main purpose in solving these problems is not to find the answers but to gain practice in using the seven stages of problem-solving. Therefore you should faithfully record your progress in each stage even though you may be able to find the answers "intuitively" by skipping stages.

1. At the local department store Mrs. Girard bought a skirt and a blouse for herself and a shirt, a pair of pajamas, a necktie, a pair of bedroom slippers, and a pair of overalls for her husband. Mr. Girard was curious to know the price of the necktie. The cash register tape listed the prices but not the names of the garments. Mrs. Girard remembered that each of the items which she bought for herself cost more than any of the items which she bought for her husband. Each of the bedroom garments, she said, cost less than any of the other garments. She also remembered that the necktie cost more than the overalls but less than the shirt. The following prices appeared on the cash register tape:

   5.25
   3.50
   2.50
   3.25
   ぐ.
   3.95
   6.50

   What was the cost of the necktie?

   29.20*

2. Which character is most talkative in the passage quoted below?

   Bernardo: Welcome, Horatio. Welcome, good Marcellus.
   Horatio: What, has this thing appeared again to-night?
   Bernardo: I have seen nothing.
   Marcellus: Horatio says 'tis but our fantasy,
   And will not let belief take hold of him
   Touching this dreaded sight twice seen of us.
   Therefore I have entreated him along
   With us to watch the minutes of this night,
   That, if again this apparition come,
   He may approve our eyes and speak to it.

   Shakespeare, *Hamlet,* I, i, 20-29.

3. A retail food corporation has decided to build a new supermarket in Boulder County, which contains five cities: Lone Pine, with a population of 5,000; Dew Valley, with a population of 15,000; Pleasanton, with a population of 30,000; Silver City, with a population of 60,000; and Creekside, with a population of 40,000. Lone Pine already has one supermarket; Dew Valley, two; Pleasanton, four; Silver City, seven; and Creekside, three. In which city should the new supermarket be built?

4. Can nine rectangles be made with six straight lines?

5. Jim works a certain number of hours a day three days a week at a certain hourly wage. George works half again as long as Jim each day two days a week at three-fourths his hourly wage. John works three times as long each week as Jim at two-thirds the hourly wage of George. If each pays the same proportion of his earnings in taxes and from the remainder banks double his tax bill, who will have the most money left to spend each week?

6. Potter has never been married. Barnes and Carter are brothers-in-law. Turnquist and O'Toole have the same marital status. Two of the five men are Californians and three are Texans. None of the men has ever been divorced; one is a widower; two (both Texans) have never been married. If Barnes is a widower what is the marital status of Carter?

7. The Smiths and the Joneses met in the Smiths' back yard one Sunday afternoon for a contest of marksmanship. The target was circular with an outside white ring, an inside blue ring, and a red bull's-eye. With a twenty-two rifle at fifty yards Mr. Smith hit the blue ring twice and the bull's-eye once. With a thirty-eight caliber pistol at fifty yards Mr. Jones got three bull's-eyes. Mrs. Smith, who was afraid of guns, hit the blue ring twice and got one bull's-eye with a bow and arrow at twenty yards. Mrs. Jones, using her husband's pistol, got one bull's-eye and missed the target twice at fifty yards.

The Smiths' adopted son, Jimmy, using his BB gun at twenty yards, hit the white ring once, the blue ring once, and got one bull's-eye. The Jones' baby daughter, Carol, was too young to compete, so Mr. Jones pointed his pistol at the target and allowed Carol to squeeze the trigger. The bullet hit the blue ring. Later Carol threw her rattle in the air and it coincidentally hit the target on the bull's-eye.

A neighbor of the Smiths, who also happened to be named Smith, stopped by to visit and stayed to try his hand at marksmanship. Borrowing Mr. Jones' pistol he hit the blue ring three times in a row at fifty yards. Then Grandfather Jones took the pistol and at twenty yards hit the white ring once, got one bull's-eye, and missed the target a third time.

Who were the better marksmen, the Smiths or the Joneses?

8. Ten men, ex-high school chums, were gathered at a restaurant for a reunion. Olson's salary was $490 a month. Two of the men had graduated from private universities; three had graduated from public universities. Blake received $1,200 a month. Wolfe's salary was $500 a month. Only three of the men had not gone to college after graduating from high school. Jones received $2.50 an hour. Morris, who had graduated from a small college, received $595 a month. All of the men who had received a higher education were paid by salary. Green, who had graduated from a public university, received $600 a month. One of the high school graduates received the lowest salary of any of the men. Black's salary was $375 a month. All of the small college graduates were paid monthly. Two of the high school graduates were better paid than one of the men who had received a higher education. The salary of one of the private university graduates was more than $1000 a month. Martin, a graduate of a private university, received $800 a month. Only one university graduate made less than $400 a month. Turner's salary was $350 a month. When the men were finished eating, Brown cashed his weekly paycheck of $200 and picked up the tab. What was the educational background of Wolfe?

9. Professor X had spent several years trying to prove the Pythagorean Theorem (which states that the square on the hypotenuse of a right triangle is equal to the sum of the squares on the other two sides) by a method other than Euclid's. One summer, while on a trip to Europe, he saw a steamship flag (pictured below) which gave him an hypothesis enabling him to solve the problem in a matter of minutes. Can you prove the theorem by the same method? The diagram of Euclid's proof, which you should *not* use, has been reproduced below for your reference.

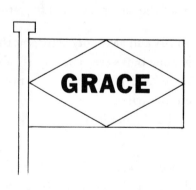
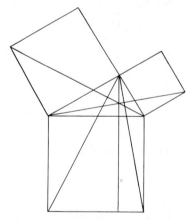

10. Obtain a copy of an unabridged edition of *Moby-Dick* and determine why the author, Herman Melville, gave the first chapter the title "Loomings." In addition to "Loomings" you should read "The Mat-Maker" and "The Chase — First Day." You may consult the dictionary but do not refer to secondary sources.

11. Determine the most powerful character in the following selection from *Middlemarch* by George Eliot (London, The Folio Society, 1972, pp. 538–43).

"Not if it had been like Casaubon," said Sir James, conscious of some indirectness in his answer, and of holding a strictly private opinion as to the perfections of his first-born.

"No! just imagine? Really it was a mercy," said Celia; "and I think it is very nice for Dodo to be a widow. She can be just as fond of our baby as if it were her own, and she can have as many notions of her own as she likes."

"It is a pity she was not a queen," said the devout Sir James.

"But what should we have been then? We must have been something else," said Celia, objecting to so laborious a flight of imagination. "I like her better as she is."

Hence, when she found that Dorothea was making arrangements for her final departure to Lowick, Celia raised her eyebrows with disappointment, and in her quiet unemphatic way shot a needle-arrow of sarcasm.

"What will you do at Lowick, Dodo? You say yourself there is nothing to be done there: everybody is so clean and well off, it makes you quite melancholy. And here you have been so happy going all about Tipton with Mr. Garth into the worst backyards. And now uncle is abroad, you and Mr. Garth can have it all your own way; and I am sure James does everything you tell him."

"I shall often come here, and I shall see how baby grows all the better," said Dorothea.

"But you will never see him washed," said Celia: "and that is quite the best part of the day." She was almost pouting: it did seem to her very hard in Dodo to go away from the baby when she might stay.

"Dear Kitty, I will come and stay all night on purpose," said Dorothea: "but I want to be alone now, and in my own home. I wish to know the Farebrothers better, and to talk to Mr. Farebrother about what there is to be done in Middlemarch."

Dorothea's native strength of will was no longer all converted into resolute submission. She had a great yearning to be at Lowick, and was simply determined to go, not feeling bound to tell all her reasons. But every one around her disapproved. Sir James was much pained, and offered that they should all migrate to Cheltenham for a few months with the sacred ark, otherwise called a cradle: at that period a man could hardly know what to propose if Cheltenham were rejected.

The Dowager Lady Chettam, just returned from a visit to her daughter in town, wished, at least, that Mrs. Vigo should be written to, and invited to accept the office of companion to Mrs. Casaubon: it was not credible that Dorothea as a young widow would think of living alone in the house at Lowick. Mrs. Vigo had been reader and secretary to royal personages, and in point of knowledge and sentiments even Dorothea could have nothing to object to her.

Mrs. Cadwallader said, privately, "You will certainly go mad in that house alone, my dear. You will see visions. We have all got to exert ourselves a little to keep sane, and call things by the same names as other people call them by. To be sure, for younger sons and women who have no money, it is a sort of provision to go mad: they are taken care of then. But you must not run into that. I daresay you are a little bored here with our good dowager; but think what a bore you might become yourself to your fellow-creatures if you were always playing tragedy queen and taking things sublimely. Sitting alone in that library at Lowick you may fancy yourself ruling the weather; you must get a few people round you who wouldn't believe you if you told them. That is a good lowering medicine."

"I never called everything by the same name that all the people about me did," said Dorothea, stoutly.

"But I suppose you have found out your mistake, my dear," said Mrs. Cadwallader, "and that is a proof of sanity."

Dorothea was aware of the sting, but it did not hurt her. "No," she said, "I still think that the greater part of the world is mistaken about many things. Surely one may be sane and yet think so, since the greater part of the world has often had to come round from its opinion."

Mrs. Cadwallader said no more on that point to Dorothea, but to her husband she remarked, "It will be well for her to marry again as soon as it is proper, if one could get her among the right people. Of course the Chettams would not wish it. But I see clearly a husband is the best thing to keep her in order. If we were not so poor I would invite Lord Triton. He will be marquis some day, and there is no denying that she would make a good marchioness: she looks handsomer than ever in her mourning."

"My dear Elinor, do let the poor woman alone. Such contrivances are of no use," said the easy Rector.

"No use? How are matches made, except by bringing men and women together? And it is a shame that her uncle should have run away and shut up the Grange just now. There ought to be plenty of eligible matches invited to Freshitt and the Grange. Lord Triton is precisely the man: full of plans for making the people happy in a soft-headed sort of way. That would just suit Mrs. Casaubon."

"Let Mrs. Casaubon choose for herself, Elinor."

"That is the nonsense you wise men talk! How can she choose if she has no variety to choose from? A woman's choice usually means taking the only man she can get. Mark my words, Humphrey. If her friends don't exert themselves, there will be a worse business than the Casaubon business yet."

"For heaven's sake don't touch on that topic, Elinor! It's a very sore point with Sir James. He would be deeply offended if you entered on it to him unnecessarily."

"I have never entered on it," said Mrs. Cadwallader, opening her hands. "Celia told me all about the will at the beginning, without any asking of mine."

"Yes, yes; but they want the thing hushed up, and I understand that the young fellow is going out of the neighbourhood."

Mrs. Cadwallader said nothing, but gave her husband three significant nods, with a very sarcastic expression in her dark eyes.

Dorothea quietly persisted in spite of remonstrance and persuasion. So by the end of June the shutters were all opened at Lowick Manor, and the morning gazed calmly into the library, shining on the rows of note-books as it shines on the weary waste planted with huge stones, the mute memorial of a forgotten faith; and the evening laden with roses entered silently into the blue-green boudoir where Dorothea chose oftenest to sit. At first she walked into every room, questioning the eighteen months of her married life, and carrying on her thoughts as if they were a speech to be heard by her husband. Then, she lingered in the library and could not be at rest till she had carefully ranged all the note-books as she imagined that he would wish to see them, in orderly sequence. The pity which had been the restraining compelling motive in her life with him still clung about his image, even while she remonstrated with him in indignant thought and told him that he was unjust. One little act of hers may perhaps be smiled at as superstitious. The "Synoptical Tabulation for the use of Mrs. Casaubon," she carefully enclosed and sealed, writing within the envelope,

I could not use it. Do you not see now that I could not submit my soul to yours, by working hopelessly at what I have no belief in? Dorothea.

Then she deposited the paper in her own desk.

That silent colloquy was perhaps only the more earnest because underneath and through it all there was always the deep longing which had really determined her to come to Lowick. The longing was to see Will Ladislaw. She did not know any good that could come of their meeting: she was helpless; her hands had been tied from making up to him for any unfairness in his lot. But her soul thirsted to see him. How could it be otherwise? If a princess in the days of enchantment had seen a four-footed creature from among those which live in herds come to her once and again with a human gaze which rested upon her with choice and beseeching, what would she think of in her journeying, what would she look for when the herds passed her? Surely for the gaze which had found her, and which she would know again. Life would be no better than candle-light tinsel and daylight rubbish if our spirits were not touched by what has been, to issues of longing and constancy. It was true that Dorothea wanted to know the Farebrothers better, and especially to talk to the new rector, but also true that remembering what Lydgate had told her about Will Ladislaw and little Miss Noble, she counted on Will's coming to Lowick to see the Fare-brother family. The very first Sunday, *before* she entered the church, she saw him as she had seen him the last time she was there, alone in the clergyman's pew; but *when* she entered his figure was gone.

In the week-days when she went to see the ladies at the Rectory, she listened in vain for some word that they might let fall about Will; but it seemed to her that Mrs. Farebrother talked of every one else in the neighbourhood and out of it.

"Probably some of Mr. Farebrother's Middlemarch hearers may follow him to Lowick sometimes. Do you not think so?" said Dorothea, rather despising herself for having a secret motive in asking the question.

"If they are wise they will, Mrs. Casaubon," said the old lady. "I see that you set a right value on my son's preaching. His grandfather on my side was an excellent clergyman, but his father was in the law: most exemplary and honest nevertheless, which is a reason for our never being rich. They say Fortune is a woman and capri-cious. But sometimes she is a good woman and gives to those who merit, which has been the case with you, Mrs. Casaubon, who have given a living to my son."

Mrs. Farebrother recurred to her knitting with a dignified satisfaction in her neat little effort at oratory, but this was not what Dorothea wanted to hear. Poor thing! she did not even know whether Will Ladislaw was still at Middlemarch, and there was no one whom she dared to ask, unless it were Lydgate. But just now she could not see Lydgate without sending for him or going to seek him. Perhaps Will Ladislaw, having heard of that strange ban against him left by Mr. Casaubon, had felt it better that he and she should not meet again, and perhaps she was wrong to wish for a meeting that others might find many good reasons against. Still "I do wish it" came at the end of those wise reflections as naturally as a sob after holding the breath. And the meeting did happen, but in a formal way quite unexpected by her.

One morning, about eleven, Dorothea was seated in her boudoir with a map of the land attached to the manor and other papers before her, which were to help her in making an exact statement for herself of her income and affairs. She had not yet applied herself to her work, but was seated with her hands folded on her lap, looking out along the avenue of limes to the distant fields. Every leaf was at rest in the sunshine, the familiar scene was changeless, and seemed to represent the prospect of her life, full of motiveless ease—motiveless, if her own energy could not seek out reasons for ardent action. The widow's cap of those times made an oval frame for the face, and had a crown standing up; the dress was an experiment in the utmost laying on of crape; but this heavy solemnity of clothing made her face look all the younger, with its recovered bloom, and the sweet, inquiring candour of her eyes.

Her reverie was broken by Tantripp, who came to say that Mr. Ladislaw was below, and begged permission to see Madam if it were not too early.

"I will see him," said Dorothea, rising immediately. "Let him be shown into the drawing-room."

The drawing-room was the most neutral room in the house to her—the one least associated with the trials of her married life: the damask matched the wood-work, which was all white and gold; there were two tall mirrors and tables with nothing on them—in brief, it was a room where you had no reason for sitting in one place rather than in another. It was below the boudoir, and had also a bow-window looking out on the avenue. But when Pratt showed Will Ladislaw into it the window was open; and a winged visitor, buzzing in and out now and then without minding the furniture, made the room look less formal and uninhabited.

"Glad to see you here again, sir," said Pratt, lingering to adjust a blind.

"I am only come to say good-bye, Pratt," said Will, who wished even the butler to know that he was too proud to hang about Mrs. Casaubon now she was a rich widow.

"Very sorry to hear it, sir," said Pratt, retiring. Of course, as a servant who was to be told nothing, he knew the fact of which Ladislaw was still ignorant, and had drawn his inferences; indeed, had not differed from his betrothed Tantripp when she said. "*Your* master was as jealous as a fiend—and no reason. Madam would look higher than Mr. Ladislaw, else I don't know her. Mrs. Cadwallader's maid says there's a lord coming who is to marry her when the mourning's over."

There were not many moments for Will to walk about with his hat in his hand before Dorothea entered. The meeting was very different from that first meeting in Rome when Will had been embarrassed and Dorothea calm. This time he felt miserable but determined, while she was in a state of agitation which could not be hidden. Just outside the door she had felt that this longed-for meeting was after all too difficult, and when she saw Will advancing towards her, the deep blush which was rare in her came with painful suddenness. Neither of them knew how it was, but neither of them spoke. She gave her hand for a moment, and then they went to sit down near the window, she on one settee and he on another opposite. Will was peculiarly uneasy: it seemed to him not like Dorothea that the mere fact of her being a widow should cause such a change in her manner of receiving him; and he knew of no other condition which could have affected their previous relation to each other—except that, as his imagination at once told him, her friends might have been poisoning her mind with their suspicions of him.

"I hope I have not presumed too much in calling," said Will; "I could not bear to leave the neighbourhood and begin a new life without seeing you to say good-bye."

"Presumed? Surely not. I should have thought it unkind if you had not wished to see me," said Dorothea, her habit of speaking with perfect genuineness asserting itself through all her uncertainty and agitation. "Are you going away immediately?"

"Very soon, I think. I intend to go to town and eat my dinners as a barrister, since, they say, that is the preparation for all public business. There will be a great deal of political work to be done by-and-by, and I mean to try and do some of it. Other men have managed to win an honourable position for themselves without family or money."

"And that will make it all the more honourable," said Dorothea, ardently. "Besides, you have so many talents. I have heard from my uncle how well you speak in public, so that every one is sorry when you leave off, and how clearly you can explain things. And you care that justice should be done to every one. I am so glad. . . ."

12. The following thirty-eight quotations describe the nature of words; almost all are similes or metaphors. Choose at least fifteen of them to analyze in solving a problem of your choice (such as, What universes of discourse are used to illustrate the nature of words? Are words master or slave? What anthropomorphic characteristics are given to words?).

1. In the beginning was the Word, and the Word was with God, and the Word was God.

John 1:1.

2. And so the Word had breath, and wrought
   With human hands the creed of creeds
   In loveliness of perfect deeds,
   More strong than all poetic thought.

Alfred, Lord Tennyson, *In Memoriam*.

3. One word is a smile, another is a look . . .

Victor Hugo, *Response à un acte d' accusation, Suite,* in Ullmann, *Semantics,* Oxford, Basil Blackwell (1970), p. 38.

4. Then he threw on deck handfuls of frozen words, and they looked like pearly pills in different colours. We saw there words of gules, words of sinople, words of azure, gilded words. When they were warmed a little in our hands, they melted like snow, and we actually heard them.

Rabelais, *Quart Livre,* in Ullmann, *Semantics,* p. 37.

5. Before writing down a word I taste it as a cook tastes the ingredient which he is going to put in his sauce; I examine it against the light as a decorator examines a Chinese vase which he wants to set against a suitable background; I weigh it as a chemist who pours into a test-tube a substance capable of blowing up every-

thing; and I use only those words whose intimate flavour and whose power of evocation and resonance are known to me.

Jean Giono, in Ullmann, *Semantics,* p. 37.

6. Words are like men.

Aristotle, *Rhetoric,* in Wagner and Radner, *Language and Reality,* New York, Thomas Y. Crowell Company (1974), p. 2.

7. Words are the tools for the job of saying what you want to say.

Bergen Evans, *The Word-a-Day Vocabulary Builder,* in Escholz, Rosa, and Clark, *Language Awareness,* New York, St. Martin's Press (1974), p. 3.

8. The words that I speak to you are spirit and life.

John Tinsdale, in "Word," *Oxford English Dictionary,* p. 3816.

9. Words are fortresses of thought. They enable us to realize our dominion over what we have already overrun in thought; to make every intellectual conquest the base of operations for others still beyond.

Sir William Hamilton, in Wagner and Radner, *Language and Reality,* p. 75.

10. Thou hast frightened the word out of his right sense, so forcible is thy wit.

William Shakespeare, *Much Ado About Nothing,* v., 2, 56.

11. But I say unto you, that every idle word that men shall speak, they shall give account thereof in the day of judgement. For by thy words thou shalt be justified, and by thy words thou shalt be condemned.

Matthew 12:36–37.

12. What a fine book one could write by relating the life and adventures of a word! It has no doubt received various impressions from the events in which it has been used; it has evoked different ideas in different places. . . . All words are expressed with a living power which they derive from the mind and which they return to it through the mysteries of a miraculous action and reaction between speech and thought. . . . By their very appearance, words reawaken in

our minds the creatures whose garments they are. . . . But this subject would perhaps require an entire science to itself!

Balzac, Louis Lambert, in Ullmann, Semantics, p. 4.

13. Words are the mysterious passers-by of the mind. . . .

Victor Hugo, Response, p. 38.

14. Present everywhere, a dwarf hidden beneath our tongues, the word holds the globe under its heels and enslaves it.

Victor Hugo, Response, p. 38.

15. [Words are] nimble and airy servitors tripping about us at command.

John Milton, Apology for Smectymnus.

16. Bright-eyed Fancy, hovering o'er,
    Scatters from her pictured urn
    Thoughts, that breathe, and words, that burn . . .

Thomas Gray, Progress of Poesy.

17. God created the world by a Word, instantaneously, without toil and pains.

The Talmud.

18. The word is the father of the act. If we are going to avoid blood then we must learn soon to curb our tongues, to end this orgy of self-indulgence in words with warheads.

Charles Osgood, WCBS Radio Report, in Eschholz, Rosa, and Clark,
Language Awareness, p. 15.

19. Look out how you use proud words. When you let proud words go, it is not easy to call them back. They wear long boots, hard boots. Look out how you use proud words.

Carl Sandburg, in Eschholz, Rosa, and Clark, Language Awareness, p. 15.

20. "When *I* use a word," Humpty Dumpty said, in rather a scornful tone, "it means just what I choose it to mean—neither more nor less."

"The question is," said Alice, "whether you *can* make words mean so many different things."

"The question is," said Humpty Dumpty, "which is to be master—that's all."

Lewis Carroll, *Through the Looking Glass.*

21. Words are women, and deeds are men.

Bodley, *Letter to James I,* in *Oxford English Dictionary,* p. 3816.

22. Place a word upon a man, and the man, shuddering, withers away and dies, penetrated by its deep force.

Victor Hugo, *Response,* p. 38.

23. The words of speech strike the guests, as a spear strikes the game or the rays of the sun strike the earth.

Kwakiutl Indian simile, in Ullmann, *Semantics,* p. 36.

24. [Words are] a perpetual Orphic song
Which rules with Daedal harmony a throng
Of thoughts and forms, which else senseless and shapeless were.

Percy Bysshe Shelley, *Prometheus Unbound, IV.*

25. Words are like a cloud of winged snakes.

Percy Bysshe Shelley, ibid.

26. [Words are] life, spirit, germ, hurricane, virtue, fire; for the name is the Word, and the Word is God.

Victor Hugo, *Response,* p. 38.

27. We next went to the School of Languages, where three Professors sat in Consultation upon improving that of their own Country.

The first Project was to shorten Discourse by cutting Polysyllables into one, and leaving out Verbs and Participles; because in Reality all things imaginable are but Nouns.

The other was a Scheme for entirely abolishing all Words whatsoever; and this was urged as a great Advantage in Point of Health as well as Brevity. For it is plain, that every Word we speak is in some degree a Diminution of our Lungs by Corrosion. . . .

Jonathan Swift, "A Voyage to Laputa," Gulliver's Travels.

28. They yawn at it, and botch up the words to fit their own thoughts.

William Shakespeare, Hamlet, iv, 5, 10.

29. "A name is a prison, God is free," once observed the Greek poet Nikos Kazantzakis. He meant, I think, that valuable though language is to man, it is by very necessity limiting, and creates for man an invisible prison. Language implies boundaries. A word spoken creates a dog, a rabbit, a man. It fixes their nature before our eyes; henceforth their shapes are, in a sense, our own creation. They are no longer part of the unnamed shifting architecture of the universe. They have been transfixed as if by sorcery, frozen into a concept, a word. Powerful though the spell of human language has proved itself to be, it has laid boundaries upon the cosmos.

Loren Eiseley, "The Cosmic Prison," Horizon, Autumn 1970.

Visionary power.

30. Attends the motions of the viewless winds,
   Embodied in the mystery of words.

William Wordsworth, The Prelude, Book V.

31. She speaks poniards, and every word stabs.

William Shakespeare, Much Ado About Nothing, ii, 1, 255.

32. The word consents or refuses; it comes running, like a fairy or bacchante . . .

Victor Hugo, Response, p. 38.

33. A large superfluous establishment of words [waiting upon us like liveried servants on a state occasion].

Charles Dickens, *David Copperfield.*

34. The world created by words exists neither in space nor time though it has semblances of both, it is eternal and indestructible, and yet its action is no stronger than a flower.

E. M. Forster, in Wagner and Radner, *Language and Reality,* p. 107.

35. One must know and recognize not merely the direct but the secret power of the word.

Knut Hamsun, in Hayakawa, *Language in Thought and Action,* New York, Harcourt Brace Jovanovich (1972), p. 102.

36. Words are wise men's counters—they do but reckon with them, but they are the money of fools.

Thomas Hobbes, in Wagner and Radner, *Language and Reality,* p. 205.

37. The craftsman is proud and careful of his tools: the surgeon does not operate with an old razor-blade: the sportsman fusses happily and long over the choice of rod, gun, club, or racquet. But the man who is working in words, unless he is a professional writer (and not always then), is singularly neglectful of his instruments.

Ivor Brown, in Gowers, *The Complete Plain Words,* Harmondsworth: Penguin Books (1971), p. 69.

38. Words are like women—seductive, inconsistent, unpredictable, frequently faithless, and full of hidden meanings.

Robert Bierstedt, *The Social Order,* New York, McGraw-Hill (1957), p. 18.

13. The following thirty-one quotations express various views concerning life after death. Choose at least fifteen of them to analyze in solving a problem of your choice (such as, What does *soul* mean? How do Eastern and Western

religious views compare? What are the basic differences between the religious and the secular views?).

1. LIFT up your eyes to heaven, and look down to the earth beneath: for the heavens shall vanish like smoke, and the earth shall be worn away like a garment, and the inhabitants thereof shall perish in like manner: but my salvation shall be for ever, and my justice shall not fail.

Isaias (Douay Version) 51:6.

2. Being once fallen into this error of "separated essences," they [men] are thereby necessarily involved in many other absurdities that follow it. For seeing they will have these forms to be real, they are obliged to assign them *some place.* But because they hold them incorporeal, without all dimension of quantity, and all men know that place is dimension, and not to be filled but by that which is corporeal, they are driven to uphold their credit with a distinction, that they are not indeed anywhere *circumscriptive,* but *definitive:* which terms being mere words, and in this occasion insignificant, pass only in Latin, that the vanity of them may be concealed. For the circumscription of a thing is nothing else but the determination or defining of its place; and so both the terms of the distinction are the same. And in particular, of the essence of a man, which, they say, is his soul, they affirm it to be all of it in his little finger, and all of it in every other part, how small soever, of his body; and yet no more soul in the whole body than in any one of those parts. Can any man think that God is served with such absurdities? And yet all this is necessary to believe, to those that will believe the existence of an incorporeal soul, separated from the body.

Thomas Hobbes, Leviathan, in Great Books of the Western World, XXIII, pp. 270-71.

3. IF a man die, shall he live *again?* all the days of my appointed time will I wait, till my change come. Thou shalt call, and I will answer thee: thou wilt have a desire to the work of thine hands.

Job 14:14-15.

4. But once gone through, we trace the round again; and are infants, boys, and men, and Ifs eternally.

Herman Melville, Moby-Dick, New York, Hendricks House (1952), p. 486.

5. The supreme Brahman in this body is also known as the Witness. It makes all our actions possible, and, as it were, sanctions them, experiencing all our experiences. It is the infinite Being, the supreme Atman. He who has experienced Brahman directly and known it to be other than Prakriti and the gunas, will not be reborn, no matter how he has lived his life.

Bhagavad-Gita, trans. Swami Prabhavananda and Christopher Isherwood, New York,
Harper & Brothers (1951), p. 137.

6. I am composed of the formal and the material; and neither of them will perish into non-existence, as neither of them came into existence out of non-existence. Every part of me then will be reduced by change into some part of the universe, and that again will change into another part of the universe, and so on for ever. And by consequence of such a change I too exist, and those who begot me, and so on for ever in the other direction. For nothing hinders us from saying so, even if the universe is administered according to definite periods of revolution.

The Meditations of Marcus Aurelius, in *Great Books of the Western World,* XII, p. 271.

7. Had I the same consciousness that I saw the ark and Noah's flood, as that I saw an overflowing of the Thames last winter, or as that I write now, I could no more doubt that I who write this now, that saw the Thames overflowed last winter, and that viewed the flood at the general deluge, was the same *self,*— place that self in what *substance* you please—than that I who write this am the same *myself* now whilst I write (whether I consist of all the same substance, material or immaterial, or no) that I was yesterday. For as to this point of being the same self, it matters not whether this present self be made up of the same or other substances—I being as much concerned, and as justly accountable for any action that was done a thousand years since, appropriated to me now by this self-consciousness, as I am for what I did the last moment.

John Locke, *An Essay Concerning Human Understanding,* in *Great Books of the Western World,* XXXV, pp. 224-25.

8. . . . if time should gather up our matter after our death and put it once more into the position in which it now is, and the light of life be given to us again, this result even would concern us not at all, when the chain of our self-consciousness has once been snapped asunder.

Lucretius, *On the Nature of Things,* in *Great Books of the Western World,* XII, p. 40.

9. Through the universal substance as through a furious torrent all bodies are carried, being by their nature united with and co-operating with the whole, as the parts of our body with one another. How many a Chrysippus, how many a Socrates, how many an Epictetus has time already swallowed up? And let the same thought occur to thee with reference to every man and thing.

Aurelius, *op. cit.,* p. 281.

10. By the Spiritual Self, so far as it belongs to the Empirical Me, I mean a man's inner or subjective being, his psychic faculties or dispositions, taken concretely; not the bare principle of personal Unity, or "pure" Ego, which remains still to be discussed. These psychic dispositions are the most enduring and intimate part of the self, that which we most verily seem to be. We take a purer self-satisfaction when we think of our ability to argue and discriminate, of our moral sensibility and conscience, of our indomitable will, than when we survey any of our other possessions. Only when these are altered is a man said to be *alienatus a se.*

Now this spiritual self may be considered in various ways. We may divide it into faculties, as just instanced, isolating them one from another, and identifying ourselves with either in turn. This is an *abstract* way of dealing with consciousness, in which, as it actually presents itself, a plurality of such faculties are always to be simultaneously found; or we may insist on a concrete view, and then the spiritual self in us will be either the entire stream of our personal consciousness, or the present "segment" or "section" of that stream, according as we take a broader or a narrower view—both the stream and the section being concrete existences in time, and each being a unity after its own peculiar kind. But whether we take it abstractly or concretely, our considering the spiritual self at all is a reflective process, is the result of our abandoning the outward-looking point of view, and of our having become able to think of subjectivity as such, *to think ourselves as thinkers.*

William James, *The Principles of Psychology,* in *Great Books of the Western World,* LIII, p. 191.

11. Yes, there is death in this business of whaling—a speechlessly quick chaotic bundling of a man into Eternity. But what then?

Melville, *op. cit.,* p. 36.

12. Great souls who find me have found the highest perfection. They are no longer reborn into this condition of transience and pain.

All the worlds, and even the heavenly realm of Brahma, are subject to the laws of rebirth. But, for the man who comes to me, there is no returning.

> There is a day, also, and night in the universe:
> The wise know this, declaring the day of Brahma
> A thousand ages in span
> And the night a thousand ages.
>
> Day dawns, and all those lives that lay hidden asleep
> Come forth and show themselves, mortally manifest:
> Night falls, and all are dissolved
> Into the sleeping germ of life.
>
> Thus they are seen, O Prince, and appear unceasingly,
> Dissolving with the dark, and with day returning
> Back to the new birth, new death:
> All helpless. They do what they must.

But behind the manifest and the unmanifest, there is another Existence, which is eternal and changeless. This is not dissolved in the general cosmic dissolution. It has been called the unmanifest, the imperishable. To reach It is said to be the greatest of all achievements. It is my highest state of being. Those who reach It are not reborn. That highest state of being can only be achieved through devotion to Him in whom all creatures exist, and by whom this universe is pervaded.

Bhagavad-Gita, op. cit., pp. 96-98.

13. . . . it must be allowed, that, if the same consciousness . . . can be transferred from one thinking substance to another, it will be possible that two thinking substances may make but one person. For the same consciousness being preserved, whether in the same or different substances, the personal identity is preserved.

Locke, *op. cit.,* p. 223.

14. For when you look back on the whole past course of immeasurable time and think how manifold are the shapes which the motions of matter take, you may easily credit this too, that these very same seeds of which we now are formed, have often before been placed in the same order in which they now are; and yet we cannot recover this in memory: a break in our existence has been interposed, and all the motions have wandered to and fro far astray from the sensations they produced.

Lucretius, *op. cit.,* p. 41.

15. . . . the soul is inseparable from its body, or at any rate . . . certain parts of it are (if it has parts)—for the actuality of some of them is nothing but the actualities of their bodily parts. Yet some may be separable because they are not the actualities of any body at all. Further, we have no light on the problem whether the soul may not be the actuality of its body in the sense in which the sailor is the actuality of the ship.

Aristotle, *On the Soul,* in *Great Books of the Western World,* VIII, p. 643.

16. THEN shall the dust return to the earth as it was: and the spirit shall return unto God who gave it.

Ecclesiastes 12:7.

17. Oh! my friends, but this is man-killing! Yet this is life. For hardly have we mortals by long toilings extracted from the world's vast bulk its small but valuable sperm; and then, with weary patience, cleansed ourselves from its defilements, and learned to live here in clean tabernacles of the soul; hardly is this done, when—*There she blows!*—the ghost is spouted up, and away we sail to fight some other world, and go through young life's old routine again.

Melville, *op. cit.,* p. 426.

18. The soul indeed of the dead lives no more, yet hath it a consciousness that lasts for ever, eternal as the ether into which it takes the final plunge.

Euripides, *Helen,* in *Great Books of the Western World,* V, p. 307.

19. Man [in early times] could no longer keep death at a distance, for he had tasted of it in his grief for the dead; but still he did not consent entirely to acknowledge it, for he could not conceive of himself as dead. So he devised a compromise; he conceded the fact of death, even his own death, but denied it the significance of annihilation, which he had had no motive for contesting where the death of his enemy had been concerned. During his contemplation

of his loved one's corpse he invented ghosts, and it was his sense of guilt at the satisfaction mingled with his sorrow that turned these new-born spirits into evil, dreaded demons. The changes wrought by death suggested to him the disjunction of the individuality into a body and a soul—first of all into several souls; in this way his train of thought ran parallel with the process of disintegration which sets in with death. The enduring remembrance of the dead became the basis for assuming other modes of existence, gave him the conception of life continued after apparent death.

Sigmund Freud, *Thoughts for the Times on War and Death,* in *Great Books of the Western World,* LIV, pp. 763-64.

20. Thou art a little soul bearing about a corpse, as Epictetus used to say.

Aurelius, *op. cit.,* p. 267.

21. Even if a man falls away from the practice of yoga, he will still win the heaven of the doers of good deeds, and dwell there many long years. After that, he will be reborn into the home of pure and prosperous parents. . . . By struggling hard, and cleansing himself of all impurities, that yogi will move gradually toward perfection through many births, and reach the highest goal at last.

Bhagavad-Gita, op. cit., pp. 86-87.

22. The parts of the whole, everything, I mean, which is naturally comprehended in the universe, must of necessity perish; but let this be understood in this sense, that they must undergo change.

Aurelius, *op. cit.,* p. 297.

23. THE eyes of the Lord in every place behold the good and the evil.

Proverbs (Douay Version) 15:3.

24. The poor body must be separated from the spirit either now or later, as it was separated from it before. Why, then, are you troubled, if it be separated now? for if it is not separated now, it will be separated afterward. Why? That the period of the universe may be completed, for it has need of the present, and of the future, and of the past.

The Discourses of Epictetus, in *Great Books of the Western World,* XII, p. 139.

25. It must not be supposed that they who assert the natural immortality of the soul are of opinion that it is absolutely incapable of annihilation even by the infinite power of the Creator who first gave it being, but only that it is not liable to be broken or dissolved by the ordinary laws of nature or motion. They indeed who hold the soul of man to be only a thin vital flame, or system of animal spirits, make it perishing and corruptible as the body; since there is nothing more easily dissipated than such a being, which it is naturally impossible should survive the ruin of the tabernacle wherein it is enclosed. And this notion has

been greedily embraced and cherished by the worst part of mankind, as the most effectual antidote against all impressions of virtue and religion. But it has been made evident that bodies, of what frame or texture soever, are barely passive ideas in the mind, which is more distant and heterogeneous from them than light is from darkness. We have shewn that the soul is indivisible, incorporeal unextended, and it is consequently incorruptible. Nothing can be plainer than that the motions, changes, decays, and dissolutions which we hourly see befall natural bodies (and which is what we mean by the *course of nature*) cannot possibly affect an active, simple, uncompounded substance; such a being therefore is indissoluble by the force of nature; that is to say, "the soul of man is naturally immortal."

George Berkeley, *The Principles of Human Knowledge,*
in *Great Books of the Western World,* XXXV, p. 441.

26. The same brain may subserve many conscious selves, either alternate or coexisting; but by what modifications in its action, or whether ultra-cerebral conditions may intervene, are questions which cannot now be answered.

James, *op. cit.,* p. 259.

27. For, behold, I create new heavens and a new earth: and the former shall not be remembered, nor come into mind.

Isaiah 65:17.

28. Again we perceive that the mind is begotten along with the body and grows up together with it and becomes old along with it. For even as children go about with a tottering and weakly body, so slender sagacity of mind follows along with it; then when their life has reached the maturity of confirmed strength, the judgement too is greater and the power of the mind more developed. Afterwards when the body has been shattered by the mastering might of time and the frame has drooped with its forces dulled, then the intellect halts, the tongue dotes, the mind gives way, all faculties fail and are found wanting at the same time. It naturally follows then that the whole nature of the soul is dissolved, like smoke, into the high air; since we see it is begotten along with the body and grows up along with it and, as I have shown, breaks down at the same time worn out with age.

Lucretius, *op. cit.,* pp. 35-36.

29. [Lord Krishna to the prince Arjuna]

> You and I, Arjuna,
> Have lived many lives.
> I remember them all:
> You do not remember.

Bhagavad-Gita, op. cit., p. 60.

30. There is one common substance, though it is distributed among countless bodies which have their several qualities. There is one soul, though it is distributed among infinite natures and individual circumscriptions (or individuals). There is one intelligent soul, though it seems to be divided.

Aurelius, *op. cit.,* p. 310.

31. ALL these things have I considered in my heart, that I might carefully understand them: there are just men and wise men, and their works are in the hand of God: and yet man knoweth not whether he be worthy of love, or hatred:

But all things are kept uncertain for the time to come, because all things equally happen to the just and to the wicked, to the good and to the evil, to the clean and to the unclean, to him that offereth victims, and to him that despiseth sacrifices. As the good is, so also is the sinner: as the perjured, so he also that sweareth truth.

This is a very great evil among all things that are done under the sun, that the same things happen to all men: whereby also the hearts of the children of men are filled with evil, and with contempt while they live, and afterwards they shall be brought down to hell.

There is no man that liveth always, or that hopeth for this: a living dog is better than a dead lion.

For the living know that they shall die, but the dead know nothing more, neither have they a reward any more: for the memory of them is forgotten.

Their love also, and their hatred, and their envy are all perished, neither have they any part in this world, and in the work that is done under the sun.

Go then, and eat thy bread with joy, and drink thy wine with gladness: because thy works please God.

At all times let thy garments be white and let not oil depart from thy head.

Live joyfully with the wife whom thou lovest, all the days of thy unsteady life, which are given to thee under the sun, all the time of thy vanity: for this is thy portion in life, and in thy labour wherewith thou labourest under the sun.

Whatsoever thy hand is able to do, do it earnestly: for neither work, nor reason, nor wisdom, nor knowledge shall be in hell, whither thou art hastening.

I turned me to another thing, and I saw that under the sun, the race is not to the swift, nor the battle to the strong, nor bread to the wise, nor riches to the learned, nor favour to the skilful: but time and chance in all.

Man knoweth not his own end: but as fishes are taken with the hook, and as birds are caught with the snare, so men are taken in the evil time, when it shall suddenly come upon them.

Ecclesiastes (Douay Version) 9:1-12.

7*2*3

PRACTICE PROBLEM WITHOUT DATA

Choose five of the problem areas listed below. Formulate a problem in each. It is suggested that your choice of problems cover a wide range of subjects and that the problems involve structure and operation analysis as well as classification. For example, your first problem might be in the realm of physical science, your second might be an artistic one, your third might involve the invention of a static or movable structure, your fourth might consist of the creation or administration of an institution or event, and your fifth might be an exercise in literary evaluation. At least one of your problems should involve a consideration of phases, in which a group solution with the assignment of individual tasks might be appropriate.

1. Compare the concept(s) of God presented in the *Old Testament* with that (those) presented in the *New Testament*. You may use your dictionary and a concordance but do not refer to secondary sources.

2. Choose a fiction or non-fiction book and determine by analysis of its contents the author's motive in writing it.

3. Pick two books or articles which express opposing views on some subject. Determine which author excels the other in some quality, such as logic, sincerity, fluency, or humor.

4. Determine whether an author, in a specific work or passage, is primarily an artist, philosopher, or scientist.

5. Imagine that clocks and calendars have not been invented and that you need a means of determining the passage of time. Develop a method of doing so by observation of the heavens. Look at the heavens themselves; do not refer to books.

6. Determine by your own experimentation the relationship between dimension and time in the operation of a pendulum.

7. Using a number of your acquaintances as subjects determine whether there is any significant relation between athletic ability and pulse rate.

8. Design and execute a work of visual art, such as a painting, drawing, mural, or piece of sculpture. You may use standard methods and materials or those of your own devising.

9. Plan and produce a work of literary art, such as a short story, poem, one-act play, or skit.

10. Create a work of musical art, such as a song, instrumental piece, or dance number. You may use any methods and devices you wish. If you are unfamiliar with musical notation, devise a symbol system of your own.

11. Execute a work of art in an art form of your own devising.

12. Design and construct a model for an improved variety of egg carton.

13. Design a machine capable of sorting coins.

14. Design a transportation system in which the possibility of accidents is minimized to the greatest degree possible.

15. Make a plan for starting and operating a business of your own.

16. Plan an advertising campaign for some real or hypothetical product.

17. Plan your finances in detail for the coming year and in general for several years after.

18. If you were a precinct captain how would you go about helping to insure the election of your party's candidates?

19. Imagine that you are a department manager in a manufacturing firm. Several members of your staff have personal differences which adversely influence their work. How would you go about correcting this situation? To make the problem specific you might create an hypothetical company, complete with its personnel, buildings, equipment, and history.

20. Develop an efficient method of teaching an infant to speak.

21. Write, or otherwise plan, a persuasive speech for some real or hypothetical occasion. Actually present the speech if you have the opportunity.

22. Imagine that you are an employer who must choose among several applicants for a position. How would you go about it?

23. Develop a system for making moral choices in your occupation and personal life. Take into account a wide range of possible circumstances.

24. Choose a problem not suggested by the foregoing items of this list.